On Demand Writing

On Demand Writing
Applying the Strategies of Impromptu
Speaking to Impromptu Writing

Lynette Williamson

International Debate Education Association
New York * Amsterdam * Brussels

International Debate Education Association
400 West 59th Street
New York, NY 10019

Activity sheets may be downloaded from www.idebate.org/handouts.htm

Library of Congress Cataloging-in-Publication Data

Williamson, Lynette.
  On demand writing : Lesson plans for applying the strategies of impromptu speaking to impromptu writing / Lynette Williamson.
    p. cm.
  Includes bibliographical references.
  ISBN 978-1-932716-45-0
  1. English language--Composition and exercises--Study and teaching (Secondary) 2. Essay--Authorship. 3. Test-taking skills--Study and teaching (Secondary) 4. Extemporaneous speaking. I. Title.
  LB1631.W396 2008
  808'.0420712--dc22
                                2008038233

Design by Gustavo Stecher, Andres Vanegas, imagenHB.com
Printed in the USA
❤ IDEBATE PRESS

CONTENTS

Speak Before You Write!

I know that I was expected to shudder in horror at the advent of on demand essays required on both high school exit exams and the new SAT I. As a 21-year veteran of the National Writing Project, I have been a devout proponent of the multiple-draft writing process. Yet, I have to admit that I was thrilled that many of the writing skills I'd been expecting of my students would finally be inspected on standardized tests. To be sure, I still believe in the writing process. Drafting and revising are tried-and-true practices for polished pieces of writing (just ask me how many times I revised this intro). However, I also find tremendous merit in being able to respond to a prompt in an organized and succinct way in a limited amount of time (just ask me how many times I dash off a quick e-mail, memo, or letter of recommendation without the luxury of editing).

We are expected to perform on demand constantly. Employers evaluate our ability to respond on demand from the moment we first meet in the job interview. Later, we need that ability for conferences, phone calls, and for presentations and meetings. What do all of these situations have in common? They all invite us to prepare ahead of time. Sure we'll never know the exact questions that will be put to us in an interview, but we'd be fools not to do a little research about the company or think through a reply to the "tell us a little bit about yourself" question. While it's not uncommon for us to pre-think before going into a situation where we may be required to speak on demand, it is uncommon for us to prepare for a situation where we may have to write on demand on an unknown prompt. This is where I turn to speech and debate students for proof that preparing for an impromptu situation—oral or written—is not only possible, it's imperative.

In addition to teaching English, I coach my school's speech and debate team. Some of my students compete interscholastically in impromptu speaking. Impromptu speaking demands that they think for 2 minutes on a randomly selected topic, then stand and deliver a 5-minute seamless speech. It requires that they develop a thesis, illustrate with specific examples from their reading, personal experience, and current events, *and* it insists that they organize their information to allow for a meaningful conclusion. So how do these kids prepare? They read. They read the novels that are assigned to them in their English classes; they read newspapers and magazines; they read their own junk-food literature, but what is important is that they read. How do they organize their thoughts in 2 minutes? They practice breaking down topics into rhetorical modes (cause and effect, comparison/contrast, process analysis, etc.), and they brainstorm and outline practice topics. How do they compose seamless analyses of a topic? They practice speaking—speaking to walls, stuffed animals, anything that doesn't have to listen and won't talk back. Then they practice for and before their friends, and finally they practice for me. All of this practice makes constructing a flawless presentation in 2 minutes possible, but they have put in hours of practice before they even draw a topic at a tournament.

Unsurprisingly, the kids who'd had the impromptu practice were the ones who not only cheered when they heard of the 25-minute SAT I essay but also scored among the highest on the test. They entered the test confident that they could think on their feet and from their seats, and they knew that they were prepared for any prompt. They had rehearsed numerous organizational strategies and had a palette of examples from which to choose. They were *prepared*.

I would like to assert that the preparation and practice of an impromptu speaker are simply the logical precursors to the impromptu writer. Encouraging students to speak before they write makes sense. Experts specializing in teaching writing to students with learning disabilities support this theory. One such research-based study found "Ultimately, the most important element is that the process of learning to think aloud with teachers and peers leads to the internalization of procedures, processes, and patterns of thinking that result in better written products. In the long run, internalization contributes to more independent learners who know and can flexibly apply the secrets that proficient writers use" (Baker, 109). Furthermore, speaking before we write adds fluidity to our expression of ideas and eventually comes to be a natural part of the writing process. Another study found that talking before writing "seemed to be particularly important because of the trouble they [students] have translating their verbalized ideas into words and sentences" (Baker, 109).

Talking through an idea is not only an efficient means of prewriting, it also allows for immediate feedback. If students can listen to a partner's response to the same prompt, they will hear alternative ways to approach topics and examples and connections that they had overlooked (Reynolds).

Nearly everyone has heard the Seinfeld joke that jabs at our fear of public speaking. He claims that most of us would rather be in the coffin than giving the eulogy. There's no denying the anxiety engendered by public speaking; this dread seems to parallel the concerns of on demand writing. Both expect impeccable verbal performance within a limited amount of time. The most common advice given to anxious public speakers is to approach the podium prepared; I believe this is a potential cure for anxious writers as well. As Eric Maisel, author of *Fearless Presenting,* states: "If we don't prepare enough—if we don't over learn our material and really master it—we're likely to have our fears realized" (65).

Students are motivated to pass their exit exams and to do well on their SATs. They prepare for these tests, memorizing rules and formulas. Purging their brains and practicing out loud are two concrete ways to give students the preparation they need and the confidence they deserve for the requirements of on demand writing.

How to Use This Book

This book is designed for teachers coaching their students for on demand writing situations. While recognizing that essays are already being assigned to students and that class time is already being devoted to coaching students on how to construct solid compositions, I offer alternative strategies that can be substituted for existing practices, thus preparing students to write effective essays with the precision and skill of sprinters rather than long-distance runners.

Each exercise is introduced by a few paragraphs of theory, explaining how the exercise will improve student performance on timed essays. Lessons follow a standard format:

Why do they need to do this?
Explains how the upcoming lesson will better prepare students for the challenges of on demand writing.

Why should they care?
Offers the teacher an explanation to give to students about why they should be glad to endure the lesson.

How long will this take?

Breaks down the time increments needed to execute part of or the entire lesson.

What will you need?

Lists what you need to photocopy or gather before the day of the lesson.

What's the procedure?

Sequences the steps of the lesson with occasional interruptions for **Hints** and optional **Lesson Extensions**.

Student handouts accompany the exercises when applicable. These handouts are also available at www.idebate.org/handouts.htm. Instructors are more than welcome to personalize the handouts.

The appendixes offer scoring guides and scored student essays that can be reproduced and used as samples and examples to illustrate for your students what high-, medium-, and low-performance essays look like.

Throughout the book, many lessons refer to a student portfolio. As portfolios are standard operating procedure in many classrooms, an attempt was made to consider the portfolio as a resource for assessing individual strengths and areas for improvement. If student portfolios aren't a part of your regular curriculum, you may want to set up each student with a writing folder that is housed in the classroom. This will allow you to save written work for use in later exercises without worrying that students will leave their papers at home under the bed.

Featured throughout the text are a series of exchanges between Peter Prickly and Mrs. Snippy. Peter Prickly is a disgruntled fellow who questions everything I teach. I know many teachers have taught him before—he wants to know why and how come, and he sometimes provides a great insight that allows me to tighten up a lesson plan. I've recorded my brief exchanges with Peter through the various chapters in hopes of offering teachers something to say in response to FAQ by students.

Many of the student handouts are adorned with a section entitled *Think About It. . . .* These questions are designed to lead students to discover *why* the exercise is beneficial. Striving to connect the theory behind the practice with the actual performance, these inquiries will serve as stimulating fodder for classroom discussions or extra credit opportunities for students who race through the exercise and ask, "Now, what can I do?"

Bibliography

Baker, Scott, et al. "Teaching Expressive Writing to Students with Disabilities: Research-Based Applications and Examples." *Journal of Learning Disabilities.* (March 1, 2003): 109. *ELibrary.* 25 July 2006. <http://elibrary.bigchalk.com>.

California High School Speech Association's Curriculum Committee. *Speaking Across the Curriculum.* New York: IDEA Press, 2004.

The College Board Online. "How the Essay Will Be Scored." 25 July 2006. <http.//www.collegeboard.com>.

Gere, Anne Ruggles, et al. *Writing on Demand.* Portsmouth, N.H.: Heinemann, 2005.

Levy, Nancy R. "Teaching Analytical Writing: Help for General Education Middle School Teachers." *Intervention in School & Clinic.* (November 1, 1996): 95. *ELibrary.* 25 July 2006. <http://elibrary.bigchalk.com>.

Maisel, Eric. *Fearless Presenting.* New York: Watson Guptil, 1997.

Reynolds, Thomas J. and Patrick L. Bruch. "Curriculum and Affect: A Participatory Developmental Writing Approach." *Journal of Developmental Education* (January 1, 2002): 12. *ELibrary.* 25 July 2006. <http://elibrary.bigchalk.com>.

CHAPTER 1

Planned Not Canned

One of the highest compliments that can be bestowed on public speakers is that they sound "planned not canned." This should be the goal of on demand writing instruction as well. We want our students to be prepared but not at the expense of employing meaningless formulas.

Before students speak or write, most of us invite them to think. Even when the topic is an unknown variable, as in the case of standardized tests, advance preparation is still feasible. A key determining factor in the SAT I's scoring rubric is the ability to craft an essay that "demonstrates critical thinking, using clearly appropriate examples, reasons, and other evidence to support its position" (The College Board). Unfortunately, one of the most common complaints of students exiting the exam is, "I couldn't think of any examples that related to the topic."

Several years ago at the state speech championships, I noticed one of my students, Julia, studying a list on a 3 x 5 card before competition. In impromptu speaking, the topics are unknown to the speaker until 2 minutes before the speech begins. For a brief moment, I thought Julia had acquired the topics in advance and was cheating. I half-jokingly asked if she was memorizing her next impromptu speech. To my surprise she replied, "Sort of." Then she revealed that what she had was a list of examples off the top of her head—topics that she was studying in school, books she was reading, recent films and songs, current events, etc. She then explained that when she drew her topic in a round, she used the 2 minutes for preparation time to connect her given topic to as many subjects on her list as she could; then, she sorted the topic areas into a progressive order and constructed a map for the audience. For years, I used Julia's "brain purge" technique to coach new impromptu speakers on my forensics team.

The same year that the SAT I debuted, I had to sit for the CLAD (Crosscultural Language and Academic Development) exam. Knowing that the essay prompts were going to be theory-based and broad, I wanted to ensure that I had specific examples to infuse into my responses. I employed Julia's method of preparation. The night before the test, I listed specific case studies that I knew well and, on another piece of paper, tiered lessons that addressed the needs of the multicultural, multi-lingual students. I committed this list to memory. The next afternoon as I scribbled my reply to the three essay questions, I was able to connect several of my planned examples to the prompts, thus I was able to name names, cite specific dates, and give meaning to otherwise lifeless prompts.

With the majority of my students facing the new SAT I later that year, I began to teach this impromptu speaking strategy to students facing on demand writing situations.

What follows in this chapter are some exercises to assist students with being planned not canned for on demand writing.

1. The Brain Purge:
Prewriting Before the Prompt

The brain purge is a prewriting activity that creates a list of potential examples before the prompt is revealed to the speaker or the writer.

Why do they need to do this?

When the topic of a speech or an essay is an unknown variable, students often assume that they can't prepare in advance. The brain purge activity offers students an opportunity to collect and focus their recent experiences into a palette of examples that they can dip into throughout the creation of a timed speech or essay.

Why should they care?

Students should care because they will never have to feel the anxiety of a blank canvas when sitting through a timed-write situation. Furthermore, the greater number of concrete examples they're able to infuse from their brain purge into their essay, the better their odds of achieving the highest score on the rubrics that demand plentiful and meaningful examples.

How long will this take?

Total time: 30–45 minutes

    10 minutes to explain the lesson and read over the student handout

    5 minutes to conduct a brain purge

    15 minutes if you plan to model the exercise as explained in Hint

    5 minutes to connect the brain purge to a prompt

    10 minutes to outline a potential essay

What will you need?

Sample Brain Purge (copies for each student)

Conducting a Brain Purge (copies for each student)

If you opt to model this exercise with the students, you will need an overhead projector and a blank transparency.

What's the procedure?

1. Explain to the class that you will give them a prewriting strategy that they can employ before they know what their prompt is so they do not have to feel anxious about on demand writing.

2. Distribute Sample Brain Purge to help illustrate the activity before you begin.

3. You may want to read the handout aloud, highlighting the fact that this is a replica of a student's response from a year ago. Reading aloud the steps and asking a student to read aloud the student responses will help distinguish the directions from the written replies. The students may also get a chuckle out of some the student samples, which are truly random.

4. Distribute Conducting a Brain Purge and give the students 5 minutes to purge their brains by listing what's on the top of their heads. Have them consider current events, recent films, books studied in class, personal experiences, and recent decisions. They may list as many items as they want—the only limiting factor is the time. You may want to help students generate their list by prompting them with questions (e.g., What was the last movie you saw? Which book are you reading in English class?)

   🔎 **Hint:** Consider modeling the exercise for your students on an overhead projector. When I do so, I scribble my brain purge on an overhead transparency while they are working on theirs. Then, I read over my list with them, noting that if I've forgotten the author of the book I'm reading or can't remember which Shakespearean sonnet we read yesterday, I would fact-check my information, so that my list is accurate and complete before I use it to prepare for a test or an unknown prompt. I then demonstrate how I would connect my random list to a particular prompt and even scratch out a rough outline for an essay. The teacher demo is particularly effective in illustrating that additions and changes can be made as the process unfolds and that the initial brain purge list is not a rigid template of examples but merely a launchpad of potential examples.

5. When the list is complete, give your students a prompt. Tell them that their essay or oral presentation will be organized around this prompt and their list.

6. Give students 5 minutes to comb their list for connections to the prompt. You can ask them to highlight or circle the suitable items on their list.

7. After students have made connections between their list and the prompt, ask them to formulate a controlling idea. This is where a return to the Sample Brain Purge is most helpful. The sample demonstrates how the initial random list was shortened to reflect just those items that the writer could connect to justice, and then the list was distilled into a controlling idea that focused on how teenagers are denied justice.

8. Give students 10 minutes to outline their potential essay or presentation. Ideally, students will have more than 1 example for each of their main points in the outline as the sample demonstrates. They may or may not have ample examples to draw from on their brain purge list. Encourage them to add examples as they work through their outline. The brain purge is a starting point, not a definitive list.

9. The exercise can stop here or be repeated with the same brain purge list and a different prompt.

> *Hint:* If you are conducting the lesson on the same day, you can ask your students to save their brain purges for the following lesson "Talking to the Wall." I've found it best, however, if each day's lesson begins with a "fresh" brain purge because these lists are subject to frequent change.

Sample Brain Purge

STEP 1: *Purge your brain; list what's on your mind.*

Consider current events, recent films, books being studied in class, personal experiences and decisions. For example:

lack of sleep	Michael Jackson
the film *300*	cell phone bill
To Kill a Mockingbird	unfair curfew
the prom	the Vietnam War
car payment/insurance	entropy
lunch	grades
war in Iraq	baseball play-offs
Interview With the Vampire	mom's birthday
school violence	*The Simpsons*
Chris Rock	

STEP 2: *Prompt (given by the teacher when the list is complete).*

Citing examples from your reading, personal experiences and observations, agree or disagree with the premise that "Justice for all" applies to teenagers.

STEP 3: *Comb your list for connections to the prompt.*

Michael Jackson	school violence
To Kill a Mockingbird	unfair curfew
car payment/insurance	grades

STEP 4: *Formulate a controlling idea or thesis.*

Teenagers are often denied justice on issues ranging from grades to violence.

STEP 5: *Outline your potential essay or presentation.*

Brain Purge Sample Outline on Justice for Teenagers

Introduction:
Personal example describing an argument with parents about Saturday's curfew.

Controlling idea or thesis:
Teenagers are often denied justice on issues ranging from grades to violence.

Main points and supporting examples (taken from the purge!):
I. High-school students are often unfairly graded
    A. grades in many subjects, such as English and art, are subjective
    B. teachers' grading policies are often unclear and inconsistent
II. In *To Kill a Mockingbird*, Mayella has no recourse against her father's abuse
    A. she was too young to be taken seriously
    B. she was too poor to garner respect
III. Many acts of school violence go unpunished
    A. hazing and harassment often go unreported
    B. punishment for reported incidents is often inconsistent

Conclusion (answers the questions, " Therefore what?" or "Now what?"):
Justice is not for all since teenagers often have no recourse when faced with unfair situations.

Conducting a Brain Purge

STEP 1: *Purge your brain; list what's on your mind.*

(consider current events, recent films, books being studied in class, personal experiences and decisions)

_____

_____

_____

_____

_____

_____

_____

_____

_____

_____

_____

_____

_____

_____

_____

_____

_____

_____

_____

STEP 2: *Prompt (given by the teacher when the list is complete).*

_____

_____

_____

_____

_____

_____

STEP 3: *Comb your list for connections to the prompt.*

_____
_____
_____
_____
_____
_____
_____
_____
_____
_____
_____
_____
_____

STEP 4: *Formulate a controlling idea or thesis.*

_____
_____
_____
_____
_____
_____
_____

STEP 5: *Outline your potential essay or presentation.*

_____
_____
_____
_____
_____
_____
_____

BRAIN PURGE OUTLINE

Introduction:

_____

_____

_____

Controlling idea or thesis:

_____

_____

_____

Main points and supporting examples (taken from the purge!):

I. _____

   A. _____

   B. _____

II. _____

   A. _____

   B. _____

III. _____

   A. _____

   B. _____

Conclusion (answers the questions, "Therefore what?" or "Now what?"):

_____

_____

_____

_____

2. Talking to the Wall: Verbalizing Ideas Before Writing

Attend any speech or debate tournament and you will see students talking to the walls before the event begins. It's sometimes best if bumpy syntax and clumsy logic fall on deaf ears. As students experiment with outlining their responses to prompts, what makes sense is to provide them with a method to test-drive their ideas in a way that builds fluency and confidence. Impromptu speaking is the most direct way to provide both efficiently. Acknowledging the fear factor of including an audience, this exercise allows students to stand and deliver to a wall.

You may want to lock your classroom door and close the blinds before beginning this exercise. With 35 students talking to the wall, an administrator dropping by for a visit or a student aide delivering a message may be more than a little confused!

Why do they need to do this?
Talking to the wall allows students to air ideas and ready them for feedback as if they were drafting an essay. This practice builds fluency and, in turn, confidence.

Why should they care?
Ask students to recall the first paragraph written on the first day following summer vacation and to compare it with an assignment written in October. They'll be reminded of how stilted and choppy their initial ideas and sentences were. By the second month of school, they could dash off the same paragraph with little concern. That progress was attributable to the comfort level and fluency born of practice. We want them to feel equally at ease with words in a timed essay situation.

How long will this take?
Total time: 20–35 minutes

  10 minutes for each round of the activity. This exercise works best immediately following The Brain Purge.

  15 minutes if you are asking students to generate a fresh brain purge and outline

  10 minutes for students to stand and deliver their outlines to the wall

What will you need?

Outlined response to a prompt generated during The Brain Purge, or you will need to conduct a new brain purge (see Hint below).

stopwatch and time cards or an LCD projector with Internet access

What is the procedure?

1. Explain to the class that this activity will allow them to verbalize the outlines generated by the brain purge.

    > 🔎 *Hint:* If you are conducting this lesson on the same day as The Brain Purge, simply have your students grab a recently generated outline and go. If you are beginning this lesson on a new day, take the 15 minutes necessary for students to generate a fresh brain purge and outline to a prompt. Since what's on their minds changes daily, so should their brain purge list. Working with a stale list is likely to stymie the writers.

2. Following the brain purge activity, ask students to grab one of their outlines and to stand facing a wall.

3. Let the class know they will be simultaneously delivering speeches based on their outlines. Another way to explain this activity is to suggest that they will be talking themselves through an essay. No conversation should be taking place—except between them and the wall.

4. Approximately 5 minutes are needed to deliver a speech the length of a 2-page essay, so let students know that you will be timing them. You can offer a prize or points to anyone who's still talking from their outline after 2 minutes—I usually stand in the middle of the room holding time cards, so as students finish talking they can turn around and check the length of their speech and record it on their outline. If you are fortunate enough to have an LCD projector that has access to the Internet, you can project a giant stopwatch on the screen by visiting:
    http://www.online-stopwatch.com/full-screen-stopwatch/

5. Reassure students that with everyone talking at once, no one but the wall is listening. Insist that once students are finished they remain standing but silently record the number of minutes their speech lasted. The cacophony should drown out the individual voices until the last couple of speakers are left standing. Those who have finished early will benefit from hearing their more loquacious classmates air their ideas.

6. The exercise can stop here or you can ask the students to repeat the exercise, attempting to beat their previous time. I prefer repeating the exercise since some of the initial awkwardness will have worn off, and they're more likely to fully develop their ideas the second time around.

> *Peter Prickly:* How is talking to a wall going to help me write better?
>
> *Mrs. Snippy:* It won't, but it sure is funny to watch! No, seriously, it will help you internalize the structure of an essay as it helps you build fluency and expand your ideas.

3. Taking It to Their Seats: Listening and Offering Feedback on an Oral Essay

During the previous exercise, you may have noticed students straining to hear what others had to say. Let them know they now have to listen—attentively—to a partner's speech. Some helpful strategies to encourage effective listening can be found in Appendix 1.

Why do they need to do this?

Hearing another student's approach to the same topic can offer reassurance that there is no single right answer to any of these prompts—answers do and should vary. Furthermore, talking through an outline with a partner will garner feedback for their ideas—even if that feedback is nonverbal. A smile or nod may encourage expansion of an idea while a puzzled look may illicit much-needed clarification.

Why should they care?

Nearly all writing prompts invite the writer to use personal observations as well as experiences. The examples they will hear from a classmate can become their "personal observations" for this essay or others that follow.

How long will this take?

Total time: 30–45 minutes

    15 minutes if you are asking students to generate a fresh Brain Purge and outline
    15 minutes for the activity
    15 minutes for the debriefing questions in step 6

If you plan to ask students to deliver their speeches in front of the entire class, you'll need 7 minutes per student speaker—5 minutes for speaking and 2 minutes for applause and shuffling back and forth from their seats.

If you plan to have them write an essay at the end, allow at least 30 more minutes.

What will you need?

stopwatch and time cards or an LCD projector with access to the Internet
seating chart or class roster will also come in handy for calling on students randomly and recording participation and/or listening points

What is the procedure?

1. Explain to the class that since answers to writing prompts do and should vary, you will be asking them to listen to how other students approached the same prompt.

2. If you are not conducting this lesson on the same day as The Brain Purge, you will want to begin with a fresh brain purge and outline to a new prompt.

3. Ask students to take the outline generated during the brain purge and sit facing a partner.

4. Let them know that they will be alternately delivering a speech—or an oral essay—based on their outlines.

5. Limit speakers to 5 minutes by offering them time signals. I usually stand in the middle of the room holding time cards, so as students finish talking they can turn around and check the length of their speech and record it on their outline. If you are fortunate enough to have an LCD projector that has access to the Internet, you can project a giant stopwatch on the screen by visiting:

   http://www.online-stopwatch.com/full-screen-stopwatch

6. After 5 minutes, ask the listener to offer oral feedback to the speaker. You may want to write the following questions on the board:
   - What was the speaker's position on the topic?
   - What was the speaker's most effective example? Why?
   - What example or idea do you think could've been expanded or explored further?

   Does this sound like peer-editing feedback? It should! The same principles that govern the expansion of oral expression apply to writing.

7. Repeat steps 3–4 for the partner.

8. Debrief with the class as a whole. Spending a few minutes addressing the following questions with students will help them realize they were actually fine-tuning the structure and content of a future essay.
   - Ask the speakers what sort of adjustments they would make before writing an essay on the same subject.
   - Ask the listeners what examples they heard that would be worth "borrowing" if they had to write an essay on the same subject. Pause to remind them that nearly all writing prompts invite the writer to use personal observations as well as experiences. The examples they just heard from a classmate can now become their "personal observations."

Peter Prickly: Wouldn't that be lying to use someone else's example or story in my essay?

Mrs. Snippy: Yes, it would be lying to pretend that the incident happened to you, so don't. Instead, do what the prompt asks and acknowledge the example as a personal observation. For example, "I have a friend who once . . . "

Lesson extensions

- The oral component of the exercise can end here, or you can invite students to perform in front of a small group or even the entire class. If and when I do this, I always give the speakers credit/no credit for standing and delivering. I also assess the audience members on their listening skills. See Appendix 1 for some tips on holding students accountable for their listening.

- Now that students have vocalized their ideas and received feedback from a partner, you can have them pen the essay. If you do have them write an essay—resist the urge to grade it. Instead, save it for the peer-evaluation exercise in Lesson 21 and the portfolio reflection in Lesson 22.

- Gradually, you can eliminate the speaking—both to walls and partners—and cut to the chase of the essay. By then, students should not only have a means for extracting examples before they begin, but plenty of practice in scratching out an outline.

As you impose more time restrictions and remove the training wheels of talking through the prompts, emphasize that the one exercise that should always be practiced before an on demand writing session is the brain purge.

Granted, students can't bring a crib sheet of notes into an SAT exam, but they can use the time spent in line outside the testing site scribbling a brain purge on a receipt or napkin. Not only is this a better use of time than biting their nails, it also will help to calm their anxieties and give them the confidence that when they see the essay prompt, they'll have something they know and understand to write about.

CHAPTER 2

Real Writers Use Roadmaps

Whether it's done with Roman numerals or bulleted with smiley faces, there's no underestimating the importance of an outline in on demand writing situation. On demand writing cannot grow organically—it cannot afford the time to trail off down side streets and stop for a Slurpee! It must have a destination in mind and a map that takes the writer—as well as the reader—there. In public speaking, we literally call this a "roadmap."

Debaters in a formal round of competition will preface their speeches by saying "To offer a brief roadmap, I will first address this and that, followed by my analysis of yada yada, and conclude with tah dah." Not only does this brief outline give the audience a sense of what's to come, it gives the extemporaneous speaker a map to follow in his speech. He knows the order of his ideas, and, most important, he acknowledges that everything that he says must be linked to that all-important conclusion—the final argument that could win him the round.

Too often, students who have been coached in formulaic essay writing have been told to place the thesis of the essay first. This only works with a great deal of prewriting and drafting and is often forced and unnatural. For proof that theses don't always come first, consult professional editorials and columns. The theses—or essential claims—are usually found at the end of the pieces. To be sure, they have a controlling idea near the beginning, but the claim that's being proven—the crux of their argument—is scaffolded and built like a spire at the apex of the essay. Students need to first recognize this, then practice it.

4. Recognizing Roadmaps: Noting the Structure of Published Essays

Recognizing the roadmap skills of professional writers is an important first step in convincing students to use roadmaps in constructing their essays in on demand situations.

Why do they need to do this?

When students see that professionals are trained to execute the same tasks that they're expected to perform, it gives real-world meaning to their work. Exposing them to the persuasive writing of syndicated weekly columnists is especially appropriate because these writers are working with space constraints and within a very limited time—much like the students writing under the shadow of a stopwatch.

Why should they care?

When I share a professional writer's work with my students and point out a similarity to what I am coaching, the students to do in their writing, I often remark, "Don't forget, this writer is getting paid to do this. We emulate her craft because we want our writing to pay off too—we want to get a good grade or a higher score."

How long will this take?

Total time: 45–50 minutes

What will you need?

Hit the Roadmap, Jack! (copy for each student)
newspaper editorial (copy for each student) or Internet access to newspaper editorial

What's the procedure?

1. Extract short editorial pieces from your local paper and secure enough copies for each of your students. Syndicated columnists like Leonard Pitts, Maureen Dowd, Richard Cohen, Ellen Goodman, and Nicholas Kristof work well as compact pieces of writing that support a thesis and can easily be studied in a class period.
2. Ask students to identify the main idea and the thesis in these columns. Stress the difference between the controlling idea—the focus of the piece—and its

thesis—the central argument being made. For instance, a piece entitled "When a Gunshot Rings Out, Does It Make a Sound?" by Leonard Pitts is a perfect example that is available at: http://www.miamiherald.com/multimedia/news/sherdavia/070706pitts.htm.

Leonard Pitts's controlling idea is America's complacency with the increase in violence against children; his thesis—which appears near the end of the piece—asserts that America needs to make preventing violence against children a top priority.

> ✎ **Peter Prickly:** I was always told to put my thesis at the beginning of my essay. In fact, in 8th grade, we had to underline it at the end of our introductions.
>
> **Mrs. Snippy:** Like a scientist, your thesis can only be asserted after you've carefully provided the data and explanation. Perhaps in 8th grade you had the luxury of drafting your essay several times to be able to anticipate what your essay would prove. But in a timed situation, it's safer and more logical to leave the complete thesis for the end of the essay where you can ensure that your previous statements and data add up to justify your final claim or thesis. You can, however, offer the reader a roadmap to follow in the beginning of your essay.

3. Using the sample below as a guide, sketch out a roadmap to Pitts's essay with the entire class via a whiteboard or overhead projector.

> **Sample Roadmap:** Leonard Pitts's column entitled "When a Gunshot Rings Out, Does It Make a Sound?" (*Miami Herald*, July 7, 2006)
>
> **Intro:** Dr. Clark's 1939 study of children and dolls led to *Brown vs. Board of Education.*
>
> **Controlling idea:** America has become complacent despite the increase in violence against children.
>
> **Supporting arguments:**
> 1. Random inner-city murders occur so frequently that they're no longer news.
> 2. Death is a way of life for children in poor, violent places.
> 3. This is not a black or white problem—this is an American problem.
>
> **Final thesis:** America needs to make keeping children safe a priority.

To reinforce that real writers employ an abundance of specific examples in their writing, ask students to extract the author's examples under each supporting argument.

> ***Sample Roadmap with Examples :*** Leonard Pitts's column entitled "When a Gunshot Rings Out, Does It Make a Sound?" (*Miami Herald*, July 7, 2006)
>
> **Intro:** Dr. Clark's 1939 study of children and dolls lead to *Brown vs. Board of Education.*
>
> **Controlling idea:** America has become complacent despite the increase in violence against children.
>
> **Supporting arguments:**
>
> 1. Random inner-city murders occur so frequently that they're no longer news.
>   *Example:* the recent murder of a 9-year-old girl in her front yard as she dug a grave for her doll received little press coverage.
> 2. Death is a way of life for children in poor, violent places.
>   *Example:* children carry guns and walk past corpses on their way to school.
> 3. This is not a black or white problem—this is an American problem.
>   *Example:* 1 in 4 persons killed in 2004 was 21 or younger.
>
> **Final thesis:** America needs to make keeping all children safe a priority.

4. After successfully roadmapping a piece as a class, give the students an article to read on their own and tell them to trace the author's route to persuasion using the student handout Hit the Roadmap, Jack!

   Sketching out the roadmaps of professional essays further reinforces the structure that we want students to internalize and also shows the truth of the claim that real writers use roadmaps. It will also illustrate the absence of a predictable formula in a well-written essay. Sometimes essays will have several supporting arguments, sometimes only one. Sometimes examples will be many, sometimes only a central cogent one. Sometimes the thesis may even occur at the beginning of the essay . . . sometimes.

Hit the Roadmap, Jack!

Instructions: Roadmap an editorial by a professional writer. Jot down the substance of the key elements of the essay by filling in the blank outline.

Intro:

_____

_____

Controlling idea:

_____

_____

Supporting arguments:

1. _____

    example: _____

    _____

2. _____

    example: _____

    _____

Final thesis:
(Hint: You'll find this near the end of the editorial.)

_____

Think About It . . .
Why is the thesis or crux of the argument left for the end of the essay rather than being stated at the beginning as you've been taught to do since 8th grade?

5. Constructing Roadmaps on Demand: Quickly Mapping Out Responses to Prompts

Being dealt a prompt and told to construct an essay in as little as 25 minutes, students may fail to realize that the secret to success is the 5–7 minutes spent mapping, not the 20 minutes spent paragraphing.

Why do they need to do this?

With only minutes to respond to an essay prompt, a student needs an endgame. If the writer has a destination in mind, the writing will be more focused and meaningful; if the writer also has a set route to follow, then the reader feels confident that they will arrive together at a logically drawn conclusion. I tell my students if they're halfway through writing an essay, and they get a bigger, better idea that doesn't fit their map—save it! In much the same way that we don't explore alternative routes to our job when we're late for work, on demand writing insists that arriving on time be our top priority. It acknowledges that some of our best thinking may come in other, more relaxed situations, but it's interested in knowing if we can plan and execute effective written communication in a limited amount of time.

Why should they care?

Nothing is worse than writing a spectacular, compelling introduction only to look at the clock and discover that only 5 minutes remain to complete the essay. Mapping out a response to an essay prompt not only ensures that writers will have a destination, it also guarantees that they will have a plan for arriving on time.

How long will this take?

Total time: 15–45 minutes

> The construction of the roadmap should only take $1/5^{th}$ of the total time allocated to the on demand writing prompt. For a 25-minute SAT I prompt, that's 5 minutes; for a 45-minute placement test, that's 7 minutes.
>
> 10 minutes to distribute materials and give a brief overview
>
> Allow 5–7 minutes for each roadmap construction

What will you need?

Constructing Roadmaps On Demand (copy for each student, or you can reproduce the handout as an overhead transparency)

copies of an essay prompt

stopwatch

What's the procedure?

1. Following at least a few exercises in Recognizing Roadmaps, tell the students that you will be distributing essay prompts and giving them only 7 minutes to write (long pause) a roadmap.

2. You may begin by conducting a brain purge—but don't allow this to absorb any of the time allotted for roadmapping. Remember, the brain purge is something that should be happening outside the time constraints of the essay.

3. Distribute Constructing Roadmaps on Demand and, as you examine the road-map templates, remind students that a good roadmap needs a final destination. You can't MapQuest unless you know where you want to go.

> 🔎 **Hint:** One year I was fortunate to have an attorney—one of my debater's dads—address my classes on how he constructs an argument for court. He stated that he always "works backward" from what he wants the jury or the judge to believe. If his thesis is the defendant is not guilty—he knows that claiming innocence in the beginning of the argument is not as effective as providing plenty of evidence and reasons that lead logically to the conclusion or thesis "not guilty." Sharing this attorney's strategy with your students may help them grasp the logic behind saving the real thesis for the end of the essay.

4. Encourage students to determine what their thesis or main argument is going to be, then work backward, filling out the rest of the map.

> ✏️ **Peter Prickly:** I was always told to sum things up in my conclusion, not to state something new.
>
> **Mrs. Snippy:** Drawing a conclusion from the information you've presented is the goal. Repeating what you've already told them creates a circle, not an essay.

5. Snag one of the retired prompts from the SAT Web site or generate one of your own.

6. Reveal the prompt to the students and set the stopwatch for 7 minutes. Students can use the template or, if you're planning to repeat the exercise, have the students use scratch paper for their roadmaps.

7. Repeat this timed procedure 2 or 3 times—each time with a new prompt. You can gradually pare down the time allotted for the roadmaps to 5 minutes. I usually spend an entire day practicing these roadmap "sprints." Then, at the conclusion of the lesson, I'm able to say—look, you've mapped out replies to 4 essay prompts in a single class—You have successfully prewritten 4 essays! Not bad for a day's work!

Lesson extensions

- If time allows, you could ask students to select a roadmap and give them 20 minutes to construct their essay based on the map. As they flesh out their essays, be mindful of your role as a coach. (See Lesson 19, Actively Coaching from the Sidelines.)
- If you do have them write an essay—resist the urge to grade it. Instead, save it for the peer-evaluation exercise in Lesson 21 and the portfolio reflection in Lesson 22.

Constructing Roadmaps on Demand

ROADMAP TEMPLATE

Intro: May be the last thing you jot down—remember you can't introduce someone until you know a little about him!

Controlling idea: Your general response to the prompt—making clear your position.

Supporting arguments: Reasons why you disagree or agree with the prompt. There's no magic number—but 2 reasons are probably plenty for a 60-minute essay that will be supported with examples.

1. _____

    example (s): _____

    _____

2. _____

    example (s): _____

    _____

Final thesis: The specific response to the prompt that draws from the reasons set forth in your essay. Be sure there's a link between the supporting arguments and the final thesis.

Think About It . . .

Why might the introduction be the last thing you plan in your roadmap?

SAMPLE ROADMAP IN RESPONSE TO A PROMPT

Prompt: Citing examples from your reading, personal experiences, and/or observations, agree or disagree with the aphorism that "Actions speak louder than words."

Intro: Children's nursery rhyme: "Sticks and stones may break my bones . . ."

Controlling idea: Words have greater influence on more people than actions.

Supporting arguments:

1. Words can incite violence or encourage peace more efficiently than actions.

   example: the speeches of Martin Luther King, Jr. and Adolf Hitler.

2. Words have a longer shelf life than actions.

   example: The words of great writers (e.g., Shakespeare) continue to influence long after the author is dead.

Final thesis: While actions may have immediate impact, words are stronger tools of communication and understanding.

YOUR ROADMAP IN RESPONSE TO A PROMPT

Prompt:

_____

_____

_____

Intro:

_____

_____

_____

Controlling idea:

_____

_____

_____

Supporting arguments:

1. _____

    example: _____

                _____

2. _____

    example: _____

                _____

Final thesis:

_____

6. Signposting: Signaling to Your Audience Where the Essay Is Going

When coaching a group of extemporaneous speakers for an upcoming tournament, I have them practice preparation more than speaking. Giving them multiple chances to draw fresh topics and to practice preparing within the time limit is often more valuable than having them stand and deliver full-length speeches. I give them topics like the ones they'll encounter at the tournament, set the stopwatch for their allotted prep time, then— rather than ask them to give a speech—I ask them to tell me what they would've told me—to roadmap how they would've broken down the topic. This allows them to experiment with different roadmaps and, most important, to analyze the expectations of various prompts. In addition, after a satisfactory breakdown of a topic, I may ask the student to return to the same topic for another timed bout of consideration, using a different roadmap.

In a speech, unlike a typical essay, the speaker is expected to "signpost" for the audience—to offer obvious indicators of where the speech is going and how the audience will get there. For example, while bad form in an essay, it's very good form in a speech to state: My first point is . . . ; my second point is . . . ; and my third and final points are. . . . For students being forced to break down a topic within a limited time, the art of signposting can be very valuable—especially, if they're later coached to remove some of the obvious phrasing.

Extemporaneous speakers draw topics that are in the form of questions. In the following exercise, the questions are modeled after those found on the writing portion of the ACT exam. They address student-friendly social issues and invite the writer to take a stance.

Why do they need to do this?
Being able to slice and dice prompts into manageable segments is a skill that instills confidence in a writer who is facing a surprise prompt. The writer "owns" the prompt after he or she has been able to break it down. Experimenting with a variety of signposting strategies for breaking down topics gives writers ready-made patterns to plug into, allowing them to focus on the real work ahead—writing.

Why should they care?
Fully addressing a prompt is a prerequisite of a passing score on any holistic rubric.

What will you need?
Signposting Strategies (copy for each student)

How long will this take?
Total time: 45–90 minutes (I recommend culminating the single-word abstract signposting activity with at least one full-length prompt, so students can see the correlation between the two.)

45 minutes for the signposting exercise on single-word abstracts

45 minutes for the signposting exercise on full-length prompts

What's the procedure?
1. Alert students to the fact that recognizing the roadmaps used by professional writers in the previous exercise was a necessary first step to creating a list of useful signposting formulas that can be used as templates in a timed situation.

2. Distribute Signposting Strategies; these have been gathered from real-world examples.

3. Model how to use the signposting strategies by selecting a single-word abstract—like "peace" or "war"—and demonstrating how you could plug the word into any of the strategies. For example:

   A. "Let's examine the causes and effects of peace," or "Let's look at how peace affects us personally, nationally, and globally."

   B. As you make your way through the strategies, note how some of the formulas work better than others for the given topic. This is crucial, for shortly students will be experimenting with which strategy best suits a given prompt.

4. Give students a single abstract noun (e.g., love, anger, wealth, success, etc.). Ask students to complete the portion of the handout entitled "Sample Signposting Strategies at Work . . . with a Single Abstract Word." Once they have completed the handout, ask them to report which formulas worked best with which topics. They will be quick to complain about the formulas that felt forced or awkward. Their complaints will serve as an excellent opportunity to remind them that, in a timed essay, they will be in control of choosing the signposting formula that works best for them and the topic.

5. Now proceed to the portion of the handout entitled "Sample Signposting Strategies at Work . . . in Response to a Prompt." Here, students will encounter topics in the form of a question.

6. Taking the first question, ask students to experiment with plugging the topic into each of the signposting strategies. Like before with the single-word abstract, they should recognize that certain formulas work better than others. For example:

   A. Examining the past, present, and future of student free speech would work much better than a process analysis approach.

   B. Plugging into the harms/benefits model would also serve the topic well, as would the real world/perfect world.

7. Ask students to select the signposting strategy they think best fits the two questions on the handout and to provide a brief roadmap of a response to each. Done first as a group effort modeled on the whiteboard with the help of the teacher, students will then have a clearer idea of how to break down their topics.

Lesson extensions

- If time allows, you could ask students to select a roadmap and give them 20 minutes to construct their essay based on the map. As they flesh out their essays, be mindful of your role as a coach. (See Lesson 19, Actively Coaching from the Sidelines.)
- If you have them write an essay—resist the urge to grade it. Instead save it for the peer-scoring exercise in Lesson 21 and the portfolio reflection in Lesson 22.

Signposting Strategies

SAMPLE STRATEGIES TO SLICE AND DICE AN ESSAY PROMPT

1. Past/Present/Future
2. Global/National/Local or Personal
3. Pros/Cons or Harms/Benefits
4. Causes/Effects
5. Process Analysis (Detail the steps and provide analysis along the way)
6. Perfect World/Real World
7. Literal/Metaphorical (Best for concrete topics)
8. Theoretically/Pragmatically

SAMPLE SIGNPOSTING STRATEGIES AT WORK . . .
WITH A SINGLE ABSTRACT WORD

Demo Word: peace	Your Word:

Demo Signposting	Your Signposting
1. Past/Present/Future Absence of peace in *past* times Struggle for peace in *present*-day society Likelihood of peace in the *future*	
2. Global/National/Local or Personal The importance of peace *globally* The need for peace *nationally* The advantages of peace *personally*	

Demo Signposting	Your Signposting
3. Pros/Cons or Harms/Benefits (Depending on your stance, you should have either more pros or cons or more harms or benefits, as shown below.) The economic *harms* of peace The humanitarian *benefits* of peace The educational *benefits* of peace	
4. Causes/Effects The *causes* of achieving peace The *causes* of keeping peace The *effects* of long-term peace	
5. Process Analysis (Detail the steps and provide analysis along the way.) Communication is the *first step* to achieving peace Compromise is a necessary *second step* Keeping promises is the *final step* to maintaining peace	

Demo Signposting	Your Signposting
6. Perfect World/ Real World In a *perfect world*, everyone lives in peace In the *real world*, most nations have been or are in conflict Using peaceful nations as models, more of the world could be at peace	
7. Literal/ Metaphorical (Best for concrete topics.) Peace *literally* means an absence of conflict Peace is *literally* the opposite of war and strife Peace *metaphorically* represents enlightenment	
8. Theoretically/ Pragmatically *Theoretically,* all of us want peace *Pragmatically,* some of us thrive without peace	

Sample Signposting Strategies at Work . . . in Response to a Prompt

Instructions: Select the signposting strategy that you think best fits the question and provide a brief roadmap.

Sample
Prompt: Do students have a right to free speech?
Signposting strategy: Real world/Perfect world
Roadmap:

- In the *real world*
    - Many high school students claim freedom of speech
        - Student newspapers and yearbooks
        - Student body elections and school board representation
    - Teachers and school administrators often curtail freedom of speech
        - On the basis of its harmful nature
        - Out of fear of bad public relations

- In a *perfect world*
    - Students could say and write what they want—but that's unrealistic
    - The guidelines for student free speech would be clear and universally upheld

Final Thesis: Therefore, the guidelines for student free speech should be clear and universally upheld.

This exercise in signposting has not only outlined a response to the prompt, it has generated a position as well. Note how the last point is a thesis in the making; changing "would" to "should" adds the assertiveness needed to stake a claim in the conclusion of the would-be essay.

1. Prompt: Is school violence on the decline?
Signposting strategy:

_____

_____

_____

Roadmap:

_____

_____

_____

_____

_____

_____

_____

_____

_____

_____

Final thesis:

_____

_____

_____

2. Prompt: Should colleges expel students for plagiarism?
Signposting strategy:

_____

_____

_____

Roadmap:

_____

_____

_____

_____

_____

_____

_____

_____

_____

_____

_____

_____

Final thesis:

_____
_____
_____

3. Prompt: Are grades a measure of student ability?
Signposting strategy:

_____
_____
_____

Roadmap:

_____
_____
_____
_____
_____
_____
_____
_____
_____
_____

Final thesis:

_____
_____
_____

4. Prompt: Should attendance factor into high school graduation requirements?
Signposting strategy:

_____
_____
_____

Roadmap:

_____
_____
_____
_____
_____
_____
_____
_____
_____

Final thesis:

_____
_____
_____

Think About It . . .

Why should you practice using several signposting strategies? Why not plug into the same one each time?

7. Extemporaneous Roadmapping: Synthesizing Nonfiction Examples

Debaters often participate in a competitive form of public speaking called extemporaneous speaking in which the speaker is given a question derived from current events and given 30 minutes to research, outline, and rehearse a 7-minute speech in response to the question. During the 30 minutes of prep time, the students consult news articles for their research. An average length news story in *Newsweek* can provide plenty of supporting information, e.g., statistics, examples, quotations from experts, to bolster the speaker's position. Since news articles are balanced, the student must scour the article in search of information that supports his or her side. For instance, if the question were: Is global warming affecting the nation's economy? The student who wants to answer "yes" has to carefully select information that agrees that global warming is taking place and that focuses on economic impacts.

Two years ago, the College Board revamped its AP Language and Composition exam to include a synthesis essay that mimics the same components of the extemporaneous speech—read through information on a topic and formulate a response to a prompt as you cite supporting evidence from the published material provided. Students are allocated 20 minutes to read the provided materials and another 40 minutes to craft an essay. I coach students to perform like the members of my extemp team—with an answer to the prompt in mind as they winnow through the published sources for supporting data.

This exercise is wonderful preparation for college-bound students who are likely to encounter this type of assignment regularly in a variety of subject areas. Their practice in a timed situation may help them to avoid the college freshman fatality—the all-nighter.

Why do they need to do this?
This exercise can be repeated frequently as a means of increasing students' knowledge of world affairs while giving them additional practice in sprinting through a roadmap in the presence of a stopwatch.

Why should they care?
Being cognizant of current events provides students with more concrete examples to draw from when faced with the standardized prompts that invite students to cite

examples from their "reading." Too often, students assume this means literature only. In this era of new skill-based standards for language arts, students are expected to read and analyze more nonfiction. This exercise not only exposes them to nonfiction, it invites them to perform one of the highest forms of analysis—synthesis.

How long will this take?

Total time: 45–55 minutes

    15 minutes to have students read an article and generate questions

    30 minutes to complete the extemporaneous roadmapping exercise

    5–10 minutes to peer-evaluate an extemporaneous roadmap

What will you need?

news magazine for each student (e.g., *US News & World Report, Time, Newsweek, The Week*). The dates and titles of the magazines need not be the same.

> *Hint:* My favorite news magazine is *The Week*, a compilation of the week's best news stories and sources. It employs several sources in crafting half-page summaries of both national and international current events in very accessible language. Class sets are available at a discount through the magazine's subscription service.

Extemporaneous Roadmapping (copy for each student)
Extemporaneous Roadmapping Scoring Rubric (copy for each student)

What's the procedure?

1. Begin with a discussion of synthesis and why it's believed to be the highest form of critical thinking.

> *Hint:* I like to start by giving students a definition of synthesis: "the combination of two or more bits of information to create something new" and then ask them, "Why do you suppose synthesis is believed to be the highest form of critical thinking?" and "What do you think a synthesis essay would look like?" If they have been practicing SAT or ACT essays, many students will recognize that these prompts invite the reader to synthesize examples to create a position.

2. Explain that they will be creating a synthesis using nonfiction examples from news magazines.

3. Distribute copies of news magazines or articles.

4. If necessary, use the table of contents to demonstrate the difference between editorial pieces and news stories. Many students may be unaware of the distinction.

5. Ask students to select a news story from a particular section (e.g., national affairs) and to read the piece, formulating a question that could be answered by some of the information in the article. Encourage them to use the words "should" "could," or "would" in their question. Modeling some sample questions might help:

   - "Could peace come to the Middle East soon?"
   - "Should UN peacekeepers be given more power?"
   - "Are organic foods healthier?"

6. Distribute copies of the Extemporaneous Roadmapping and have students fill in the source and a question, tuck the paper inside the magazine next to the article, and pass the magazines back to you. Do not have them write their name on the handout; these questions will be redistributed randomly to other students.

7. If students are struggling with crafting appropriate questions, you could screen them by asking students to read their questions aloud before handing them over to you—this would allow you to suggest changes and, one hopes, the others listening would alter their questions based on corrections. If time does not allow for this, a quick peek at the questions as you redistribute the magazines and questions would give you a chance to intercept and change any truly faulty questions (e.g., Is gasoline expensive?).

8. Randomly redistribute the magazines (with the questions still tucked inside) and give students a total of 30 minutes to do the following:

   - Read the article, highlighting or underlining information that pertains to their specific question.
   - Respond to the question simply (e.g., "Yes" or "No") or with a qualified answer ("Only if . . . " or "Not now, but possibly in the future . . . ").
   - Outline support of their answer, extracting information from the article and using the template on Extemporaneous Roadmapping.
   - Answer the final question "Therefore what?" or "Now what?," which will assist them in crafting a final thesis statement.

   Students can then swap roadmaps and score one another's maps using the Extemporaneous Roadmapping Scoring Rubric.

> 🔎 ***Hint:*** While it's valuable for students to receive peer evaluations, noting their strengths and areas for improvement, you may not feel confident in the accuracy of their numerical judgments. If this is the case, you can reassure students that while their score sheets may reflect a variety of points, you will only be recording credit/no credit for the exercise.

9. If time allows, you can call on students to orally respond to their questions, either from their seats or from the front of the room, and you can score them on their replies. The more they hear specific evidence being cited to support claims, the more they begin to internalize this as a natural and necessary pattern.

10. Whether it's peer evaluation or teacher evaluation, it's best if the score sheets are returned to the students at the end of the lesson so they can reflect on their effective use of examples. You can always collect the scoring sheets again as the students exit the classroom if you haven't had a chance to record the scores in the grade book.

Lesson extensions

- Once students have rehearsed this lesson, it could easily become one of your favorite lesson plans for use by a substitute teacher. It keeps students reading and writing, and, upon your return, an entire period can be devoted to developing their synthesis arguments—either orally or in writing—as you catch your breath.

- Collect the completed Extemporaneous Roadmapping sheets from the students at the end of the period and save them for one of the options in Lesson 11: Transforming Inductive Thinking into Deductive Writing.

Extemporaneous Roadmapping

PART I: DEVELOPING THE QUESTION

Instructions: Fill in the source and a question, tuck the paper inside the magazine next to the article, and pass the magazines back to your teacher. Do *not* write your name on the handout.

The Source (author of article, title of article, name of magazine, date):

_____

_____

_____

The Question:

_____

_____

_____

PART II: DEVELOPING THE ANSWER

Instructions: Read the article, highlighting or underlining information that pertains to the specific question. Then:

1. Respond to the question with a simple answer (e.g., "Yes" or "No") or with a qualified answer ("Only if . . . " or " Not now, but possibly in the future . . . ").
2. Outline support for your answer, extracting information from the article.
3. Answer the question "Now what?" or "So what?," which will assist you in crafting a final thesis statement

Your Answer:

_____

_____

_____

_____

Reasons why your answer is correct:

1. _____

_____

Proof (expert quotes, facts, and examples) from the article:

_____

2. _____

_____

Proof (expert quotes, facts, and examples) from the article:

_____

3. _____

_____

Proof (expert quotes, facts, and examples) from the article:

_____

4. _____

_____

Proof (expert quotes, facts, and examples) from the article:

_____

Final thesis (answers the question "Therefore what?" or "Now what?"):

_____

_____

Think About It . . .
Why is it impossible to predict exactly how many reasons you should have to support an answer to a prompt?

Extemporaneous Roadmapping Scoring Rubric

Name: _____

Topic: _____

	Score
Preparation (completed template)	
Proof (specific references to information from the news article)	
Prompt Development (reasons and proof clearly connect to the language of the prompt)	
Total	/15

Scoring

5-Exceptional! *4*-Accomplished *3*-Competent *2*-Incomplete *1*-Missing

8. Collecting Aphorisms: Infusing Notable Quotations into Timed Essays

Another strategy employed by impromptu speakers striving to sound planned and not canned is the infusion of quotations into their speeches. It's not uncommon to find quotes from John F. Kennedy or maybe even Rousseau sprinkled among their analyses of current economic policy or a critique of U.S. energy consumption. Committed to memory, these quotations constitute a resource library that speakers can draw on to support a claim or add credibility to an otherwise bland speech.

As a coach, I encourage my student speakers to latch onto catchphrases from their studies in their English and history classes and to make connections between their debate cases or impromptu topics. For example, if they are reading Shakespeare's *Macbeth*, it would serve them well to memorize the line, "Fair is foul and foul is fair" as a ready-made example of paradox that could be applied to a debate on gun control just as easily as a speech on divorce rates. Or, borrowing the line, "It's better to be feared than loved" from Machiavelli, they could offer analysis of a world leader's foreign policy or a pop celebrity's battle with the paparazzi.

Not until I "caught" my speech team members employing this tactic on their timed essays did it dawn on me that students struggling with on demand writing prompts could also extract proofs from literature.

Why do they need to do this?
Although, as Voltaire said, "A witty saying proves nothing," there's no denying that a well-placed quote can lend even the most lackluster essay a spark that would qualify as a specific detail required on most rubrics.

Why should they care?
Committing a collection of quotations to memory builds a personal library of accessible aphorisms that can be employed when dry for an example or idea. Students leave this activity with a handful of clever quotes that can be folded into a timed essay or woven into an impromptu speech.

How long will this take?
This exercise can be conducted as an overnight homework assignment or as part of an ongoing semester project.

What will you need?

Collecting Aphorisms (copy for each student)—you can modify this handout before photocopying or ask students to fill in the blanks after you've distributed the papers. A list of the current readings in English or history class.

What's the procedure?

Decide whether you want your students to keep an ongoing aphorism journal that covers a semester's worth of reading or whether the journal will simply record meaningful quotes from a single work.

> 🔍 *Hint:* I prefer giving students a single theme to focus on as they read a work of literature in search of notable quotations or aphorisms. For instance, when they read *Oedipus Rex*, I ask them to watch for lines that refer to truth. At the end of play, I may ask them to select 4 lines that they discovered and to write those lines in their journal. At this point, I can ask them to commit those aphorisms to memory for use on an in class essay, or I can ask them to use one of the aphorisms to generate a prompt to write about or for another student to respond to (see Lesson 12: The Prompt Generator).

1. Distribute Collecting Aphorisms. If you haven't already modified the handout to fit the literature being studied, do so with the class filling in the blanks.
2. After the class has read over the handout and you have clarified themes and deadlines, alert students of two significant changes in the way they should approach the text they are about to read:
    *   They will be expected to read their next assignment "actively" rather than passively. It will no longer be enough for them to merely read the words—they must respond to the words. Recommend that they use Post-It notes or (if your school district permits) mark in their texts with a pencil when they encounter quotable lines that connect to particular themes or topics the class is studying.
    *   They will be expected to memorize some of these lines. This warning serves to keep their extractions compact yet full of meaning—the very nature of a good aphorism. They may ask about shortening a lengthy quote, to which you can reply—"I have three dots for you . . . "

> ✎ **Peter Prickly:** Do the quotes have to be verbatim?
> **Mrs. Snippy:** Small slips will be forgivable.

Committing the quotations to memory builds their personal library of accessible aphorisms that they can pull from when needed for an illustration or idea. What is important is for students to leave the text with a handful of clever quotes that can be folded into a timed essay.

3. To achieve the goal of having students memorize some aphorisms, present this task as a quiz on the day after they were to have completed the text. See the following sample assignment that illustrates the procedure:

> The truth hurts. Nobody knows this better than Oedipus. As you read the play *Oedipus Rex*, make note of lines that address the nature of truth. Transcribe these lines and their page numbers into your aphorism journal. After we have read the play, you will be expected to recount *from memory* 4 of the lines from your journal. This will count as a quiz.
>
> Then you will respond to a prompt on truth in a timed essay in which you will more than likely be tempted to use some of your memorized quotes—do not resist the temptation—use them!

Lesson extensions

- As students make their way through the literary work or text, ask them to pause and reflect on one of the aphorisms in their journal. If you prefer, you can suggest an aphorism for everyone's journal to ensure that all students have an important quote that you know will come in handy on their essays.
- I have a colleague who has her students maintain a writers' notebook in which an entire section is devoted to collecting aphorisms from a variety of sources. As she grades these notebooks on a per-page basis, she asks for a certain number of pages of aphorisms by her semester deadline.
- After the students have read the literary work or text, distribute a prompt on the chosen theme. For example, in the case of the sample assignment on *Oedipus Rex*, the prompt would relate to "truth." Before the students begin responding to the prompt, give them a generous 10 minutes to transcribe their 4 memorized aphorisms on the back of the prompt, reminding them that these quotes will be graded as a quiz.

Collecting Aphorisms

Instructions: As you read _____ make note of lines that address the theme of _____. Transcribe these lines and their page numbers onto paper to create an aphorism journal.

After we have finished reading the text you will be expected to recount *from memory* 4 of the lines from your journal. This quiz will take place on: _____ .

On _____ , you will respond to a prompt on the theme of _____ in a timed essay in which you will more than likely be tempted to use some of your memorized quotes—do not resist the temptation—use them!

Why do we have to memorize these quotations?
Committing the quotations to memory builds your personal library of accessible aphorisms that you can pull from when you need an example or idea.

What if we locate a really long quotation and are afraid of being unable to memorize it?
You may use ellipses (. . .) to shorten the line so it's more manageable to memorize.

Think About It . . .
Identify three situations where having a memorized aphorism at the ready may come in handy.

9. Eliminating B.O.: Removing the Blatantly Obvious from the Roadmaps

Probably the most evident stylistic difference between a speech and an essay is that a speech contains blatant references to its own structure. The roadmaps are often announced—"First I will discuss . . . then I will investigate . . . " and the examples are often labeled as such—"Another example of this theory is . . . " or "This example proves that . . . " As writing instructors, however, we red-pencil this verbiage out of essays as unnecessary padding that interferes with sophisticated style. How then do we train students to use roadmaps without stating the obvious in their essays?

While working in a college writing lab, another teaching assistant and I struggled with a proofreading symbol for these wordy moments in student essays. Scribbling "wordy" or "redundant" seemed tedious and ineffective. That's when we devised the proofreading mark "B.O."—for "Blatantly Obvious." When students saw this in their margins—or worse yet read comments like "Your B.O. is stinking up your style!" they took notice. I use this proofreading mark to this day for its impact. I also post a list of blatantly obvious phrases on my classroom wall. I emphasize that these phrases are fine in speeches, but, when making the transition to an essay, they should be eliminated like a bad smell.

Why do they need to do this?

Phrases that beg the question or pad an answer are unnecessary and detract from the impact or urgency of a statement. "It feels to me as if students should be given greater freedom of speech on campus" softens the cogency of asserting, "Students should be given greater freedom of speech on campus."

Why should they care?

Students interested in reaching the upper end of the scoring rubrics need to heed their stylistic choices as well as their structural ones. I've yet to read a high-end essay released by the College Board that features redundancy and B.O. In fact, every year, I challenge my students: if they can find a professional columnist who uses the phrase "in conclusion," I will award them extra credit. To date, I've had to dole out one portion of extra credit—to a sly student who inserted the line into his own weekly column for the local paper.

How long will this take?

Total time: 50 minutes

> 30 minutes should be adequate time to expose them to the list of Blatantly Obvious phrases and to have them edit the mini-essay on the student handout. Allow another 20 minutes to self-edit a previously written essay as explained in step 6.

What will you need?

Removing B.O. from Your Writing (copy for each student)
editorial page of a newspaper or classroom textbook (copy for each student)
writing portfolios or previously written essays (optional)

What is the procedure?

1. Tell the class that not all words add meaning, and that today you are going to alert them to words and phrases that actually "stink up" the clarity of their essays.

   > 🔎 *Hint:* I like to begin class with a long string of B.O. (e.g., "It behooves me to inform you that today I am planning to introduce to you a lesson that when presented will clarify to you the importance of being really, really clear when you write words that will be read."), then I ask the students "What did I just say?" followed by "What effect did all those words have on the clarity of my message?"

2. Distribute Removing the B.O. or post the list of Blatantly Obvious phrases on your board.

3. Generate a discussion with students, asking them "Why are these phrases unnecessary in a piece of writing?"

4. Distribute the editorial page of a newspaper or ask students to open a textbook to an essay and challenge them to find these phrases. They won't—usually! You can extend to them the same challenge I've offered to my students—just be wary of the wily student columnist!

5. You may want to extract a few lines of the text being studied and infuse some of the Blatantly Obvious phrases to demonstrate how unnecessary the phrases would be.

6. Direct students' attention to the section of the handout titled Test Your B.O. Sensors and challenge them to eradicate all of the B.O. in the mini-essay.

Lesson extensions

- If students have their writing portfolios or one of their recent writing assignments handy, you could ask them to scour the piece for B.O., then award points for the phrases they share aloud with the class.
- If you have extra time or the need for a homework assignment, ask students to write a mini-essay based on one of their roadmaps in Lesson 5.
- Ideally, their next piece of writing—even if it's only a paragraph—should be scrutinized for any lingering B.O. It's a very easy and effective element of style to assign to peer editors.

Removing the B.O. from Your Writing

ELIMINATE THESE B.O. (BLATANTLY OBVIOUS) PHRASES FROM YOUR WRITING

"I feel . . . "
"I think . . . "
"I believe . . . "
"I will show . . . "
"In this essay . . . "
"In my opinion . . . "
"I agree/disagree . . . "
"It seems to me that . . . "
"In conclusion . . . "
"We will examine . . . "
"I have proven that . . . "
"Another example is . . . "
"This is true/false for three reasons . . . "

> ✐ **Student:** How will the reader know that this is my opinion if I don't say that it's my opinion?
> **Teacher:** Who else would the opinion belong to? You wrote the essay; you own the ideas.

TEST YOUR B.O. SENSORS

Instructions: Sniff out the B.O. phrases in the following mini-essay. Draw a line through any B.O. and add additional words when necessary to maintain sentence sense.

Do students have a right to free speech? In this essay I will show that there is a differ-

ence between free speech for students in the real world and in a perfect world.

In the real world, many high school students claim to have freedom of speech. Students publish their views in on-campus publications like student-run newspapers and yearbook publications. Another example is when students represent the student body as officers or as school board representatives. I think that these positions give students a voice in how the school is run, but I don't agree that these opportunities necessarily grant students free speech.

Teachers and school administrators often curtail freedom of speech. When principals and teachers find student expression potentially harmful, I feel that they must intervene. For example, if a student wears a T-shirt advertising beer or making a racial slur, I agree that the school should squelch the speech. Sometimes a school will react negatively to student speech if it expresses something that may be bad for the school's public relations. For example, if there are lousy leaky bathrooms on campus, the school may be struggling to fix them and not appreciate a student's editorial column critiquing the quality of the bathrooms on campus.

In a perfect world, students could say and write what they want. Perhaps a more realistic model of perfection, however, would be one in which the guidelines for student free speech would be clear and universally upheld. If students were clear about the limits of their free speech, they would be less likely to breech the restrictions and more likely to express themselves within the guidelines. If the consequences for

hurtful speech were the same from campus to campus, then students would have a

greater sense of fairness and feel less threatened by limits on their free speech.

In conclusion, the guidelines for student free speech SHOULD be clear to all stu-

dents and universally upheld by school administrators.

Think About It . . .
If you were delivering the same information as a speech to be heard rather than an essay to be read, why might you want to leave in the B.O.?

CHAPTER 3

Thinking Inductively, Writing Deductively

Our brains take in specific information and through induction draw conclusions. Touching a flame tells us that fire is hot; biting into an unripe strawberry allows us to conclude that green strawberries can be tart. Inductive thinking allows us to make connections—to make sense of our world. When we're trying to persuade someone of our findings, however, we reverse these organic processes and begin with a general premise (e.g., Don't touch that!—the pan is hot!), Beginning with a general premise and moving toward specific supporting examples is known as deductive reasoning; it is more sophisticated than induction and relies on artful construction.

Deduction is a complicated and often unnatural procedure for student writers. Most students are apt to simply record their inductive thought processes without giving consideration to converting their ideas into a persuasive, deductively arranged argument. If, for instance, a student is reading a novel and every time the character named "Peter" appears and acts selfishly, the student may inductively arrive at the claim: the character Peter is selfish. When asked to write a character analysis of Peter, the student may simply present a series of examples of Peter acting selfishly without making a claim about Peter's selfishness. I call this the "clothesline essay"—a series of examples strung together without developing an argument (e.g., Peter acts selfishly in chapter 3. Another example of Peter acting selfishly comes at the end of the book, etc.). An English teacher—or anyone reading the student's essay—would expect the essay to stake a claim, then support it with examples from the book (e.g., Peter acts selfishly as a defense mechanism. This is illustrated in chapter 3 when . . .).

To help students develop their ideas logically and avoid the "clothesline essay," we can aid them to first recognize the difference between inductive and deductive thinking, then assist them in discovering how they typically organize their thoughts when faced with a particular prompt. For instance, if given the prompt "Is it good to be selfish?," someone may immediately respond with a general premise and deductively declare: "No, it is never a positive attribute to be selfish." Someone else, however, may immediately reply with a specific example and inductively reason: "My brother Peter was very selfish toward me when I was little, but his unwillingness to share increased my self-reliance and independence." Once students can recognize their inductive and deductive patterns of thought, they are more likely to be able to effectively manipulate the order of ideas for a formal essay.

10. Brain Lather: Quick Writing to Diagnose Inductive or Deductive Thinking

When I first assigned this exercise, I told my students that they were going to have an opportunity to blather on paper for 7 minutes. When one student (probably Peter Prickly) asked what I meant by "blather," another student replied that it sounded like "brain lather"—a metaphoric foaming at the brain. His description captured the essence of a quick write—to pen thoughts without attention to mechanics or structure. This spontaneous writing is probably the best method for students to discover how their brain constructs arguments naturally. Understanding this natural process is the first step in manipulating it for on demand writing situations.

Why do they need to do this?

When organizing and writing an essay, students generally articulate the claims first followed by supporting examples. Many students have been well trained since grade school to put a topic sentence at the beginning of a paragraph and to tuck in the concrete examples below it. What they haven't been taught, however, is that this deductive reasoning can only come after they have formulated their arguments inductively. This exercise will help them see this organic process and guide them toward manipulating it for on demand writing situations.

By completing this diagnostic quick write, some students discover that they will immediately conjure a specific example in response to a prompt—this diagnoses them as an inductive thinker, alerting them to the fact that they must concentrate to reverse their natural structure when constructing a formal argument for an essay. Those students who respond naturally with a general claim are on their way to deductive reasoning but often need coaxing to remember to provide specific supporting examples.

Why should they care?

When a piece of writing is holistically scored, the evaluator can easily skim the essay's content if the body paragraphs begin with clear claims. Paragraphs that begin with an assertion like "Money is more important than love" score points for critical thinking; whereas paragraphs that begin with "Another example of money's importance to love is when . . . " lose points for lackluster reasoning as well as awkward syntax.

How long will this take?

Total time: 50 minutes.

15–20 minutes for the quick write and diagnosis of inductive thinking

20–30 minutes for reviewing the handout and asking students to complete the worksheet

What will you need?

What Kind of Thinker Are You? (copy for each student)

timer

What's the procedure?

1. Announce to students that today they will be discovering how their brains are hardwired to think and be shown ways of manipulating this hardwiring to improve their essay structure. (This introduction will intrigue them and they may not even notice that you are scrawling an essay prompt on the board and about to make them write.)

2. Tell students that you will give them a prompt and expect them to complete a "quick write" in which they write nonstop for 7 minutes.

3. Assure them that this writing will not be assessed for grammar, spelling, or structure, but that they will be conducting a self-assessment of their writing later.

4. Set the timer and ask students to respond to a prompt that has been constructed as a question. Sample prompts that work well include:

   Are grades an accurate measure of students' abilities?

   Are cell phones a distraction in the classroom?

   Do spirit rallies improve student morale?

5. Remind students to keep their pen or pencil flowing across the page for the full 7 minutes—there is no need to pause to correct errors or to think of precisely the right word.

   ✒ **Peter Prickly:** What if I don't have any good ideas?
   Mrs. Snippy: Then write down what you do have. This exercise is to assess your thinking not your writing.

6. After the 7 minutes have elapsed, ask the students to read what they wrote and to underline any concrete detail or specific examples. If students are unsure

what constitutes a concrete detail, you could read aloud a sample paragraph from the student handout and identify the concrete examples.

7. Then ask students if they have concrete detail or specific examples in their first two sentences. If so, ask them to draw a triangle on the top of their paper. The tip of the triangle represents specific examples while the base of the triangle represents the general conclusions being drawn.

8. If they don't have concrete detail or specific examples in their first two sentences, ask them to draw an upside down triangle on their paper. This indicates that their general claims were made first and that specific examples—the tip of the triangle—will follow to support the claims.

9. Emphasize that neither triangle is a badge of shame or honor but merely denotes a difference in the way they constructed their argument. The upright triangle represents inductive thinking, while the inverted triangle suggests deductive reasoning.

10. Distribute What Kind of Thinker Are You? and review the first two examples, stressing the fact that early man, just like young children, learned inductively but then shared that knowledge deductively with those less experienced. The lifeguard who barks "Walk, don't run!" at the children cavorting around the pool didn't need to fall and crack her skull to know that running around a concrete pool could lead to injury.

11. Ask students to read the sample paragraphs and to assess whether they are constructed inductively or deductively and to determine how they knew that.

> *Peter Prickly:* Both of those paragraphs are pretty good. Why can't we write inductively in our essays?
>
> *Mrs. Snapback:* You can, but in a timed essay the deductively constructed paragraph is easier to scan and indicates clear organization to the evaluator. Your induction can be tucked inside the paragraph.

12. When students reach the *Think About It . . .* question on the handout, they may need some coaching to remember that when they're writing an on demand essay for the SAT I or the ACT test, they're actually persuading the evaluator to accept their argument; this requires making claims first, then offering supporting data to tell the reader what to make of the examples. Otherwise the data are lost before the claim can be made.

What Kind of Thinker Are You?

Making sense of the world requires logic. Even earliest man employed logic to arrive at conclusions about his universe.

INDUCTIVE REASONING goes from the specific to the general and is the most common and primitive type of reasoning. For example:

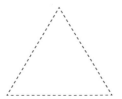

evidence
Org ate the red plant and died that night
Ugh ate the red plant and died that night
Ick ate the red plant and died that night
assertion
The red plant killed them
conclusion
The red plant is deadly

Sometimes—if we're smart or lucky— induction leads to deduction.

DEDUCTIVE REASONING goes from the general to the specific. For example:

major premise
The red plant is deadly
minor premise
Ur ate the red plant
conclusion
Ur will die

The above example is also referred to as a syllogism.

Instructions: Writers use both inductive and deductive reasoning to express their ideas. See if you can determine which of the following paragraphs is inductive and which is deductive.

Prompt: Are grades an accurate measure of students' abilities?

Paragraph 1: Every once in a while there's a boy in history class who knows everything about the trade routes of Russia, but when test time comes around Joe Schmart scores a "D" while the class averages an 85%. School smarts are completely different from a student's true potential and talent. Grades fairly assess someone's talent only if he or she is committed to playing the game of being a good student.

Is the above paragraph inductive or deductive?
Why?

_____

_____

_____

Paragraph 2: Students who are very intelligent and who have high potential might receive poor grades even with a large brain capacity. Grades test laziness, punctuality, neatness, and ability to work under pressure, therefore testing a student's performance rather than intellect. My neighbor receives C's yet he scored a 2200 on his SAT's; I studied for four months for my SAT's and barely scored a 2000, yet I maintain a 4.0 GPA at school.

Is the above paragraph inductive or deductive?
Why?

_____

_____

_____

Think About It ...
Why is it that even though our brains are hardwired to think inductively, when we write essays, the reader expects our arguments to be constructed deductively with the general claim coming before the supporting evidence?

11. Data/Warrant/Claim: Transforming Inductive Thinking into Deductive Writing

When students were first introduced to the brain purge exercise in Chapter 1, they were collecting potential examples for use in an essay. The examples, or data, were assembled first, then the prompt was distributed, and bits of data were selected that would help support the writer's response to the prompt. This very primitive procedure follows Steven Toulmin's model for inductive reasoning—data, warrant, and claim. The claim, or thesis, is drawn at the end of data collection and analysis. However, as we know, most arguments—whether in the form of a debate case or the body paragraphs of an essay—begin with general statements followed by supporting details. This next exercise helps students recognize the difference between data and claims so that they can rearrange them for a formal essay.

Why do they need to do this?

Discerning an opinion or assertion from a fact or bit of data is essential not only for writers, but for readers as well. This type of distinction is a frequent question on the reading portion of standardized tests.

Why should they care?

Warrantless claims are illogical and fail to earn points for critical thinking. A string of examples without warrants linking them to a claim is meaningless and ineffective. Identifying data, warrants, and claims is the first step in making certain that each argument a student constructs has all three essential elements of an argument.

How long will this take?

Total time: 40–70 minutes

I often have my students complete the student handout Data/Warrant/Claim as homework. It takes about 20 minutes.

Allow another 20–30 minutes for discussion and comparison of their answers and another 20 minutes for paragraph construction.

What will you need?

Data/Warrant/Claim (copy for each student)
completed Extemporaneous Roadmapping handouts from Lesson 7 (optional)
editorials or research-based essays (optional)

What's the procedure?

1. Remind students that arguments consist of data (examples), warrants (reasons), and claims (assertions).

> 🔎 **Hint:** I like to put the terms "data," "warrant," and "claim" on the board and then ask students to chime in with alternative terminology that they may have heard or used to refer to these components as they are referenced in an essay. For example, at our high school, all freshmen are exposed to a Jane Schaefer writing unity that labels the parts of the essay as "concrete detail," "commentary," and "thesis"—different terms for essentially the same elements : data, warrant, claim. As I collect these terms from students, I write them on the board, so everyone can see the various, interchangeable terms. I prefer to work with the terms "data, warrant, claim" because they stem from Toulmin's theory of logical argument—a theory that is nearly universally accepted in college composition courses and textbooks.

2. Distribute Data/Warrant/Claim. Review the directions and read aloud the warrants and claims that can be drawn from the example. Emphasize how different claims can be drawn from the same data—that's why there are so many opinions in the world!

3. Allow 20 minutes for students to complete the handout, filling in the missing warrants and claims.

4. After time is up, ask students to share their responses to the first data (the data that could be used in an essay responding to the prompt about grades). Compare the various warrants for the same data.

> ✏️ **Peter Prickly:** What if I have the same warrant as someone, but a different claim. For instance, I agree that teachers inflate grades, but I think it's because teachers have gotten lazy.
>
> **Mrs. Snippy:** It's only natural for people to vary in their claims—just be sure you can support them when asked. For instance, be prepared to prove that teachers are lazy!

5. Then invite students who had the same warrants to compare claims.

6. Read aloud the two model paragraphs located on the last page of the student

handout. These paragraphs were created from the data, warrants, and claims made on the first grid. Emphasize that these paragraphs demonstrate the rearrangement of the data, warrant, and claim to logically construct an argument.

7. Ask students to select one of the topic areas from the grid—preferably on an issue that struck a nerve for them—and to use the warrant as a topic sentence for a paragraph in which they use the data and arrive at the claim at the end. If they need to add sentences to link the material together, that's fine. Allow 20 minutes for this paragraph construction.

Lesson extensions

- The completed grid can be used as a resource for more paragraph construction for homework or another day in class.
- It may be helpful to return to Lesson 7, Extemporaneous Roadmapping, encouraging students to apply the data/warrant/claim model by filling in their examples first, then their supporting ideas as they map out a response to a prompt.
- To emphasize the real-world application of this sort of paragraph construction, distribute copies of editorials or research-based essays and ask students to find the data, warrants, and claims. They will begin to see that real writers don't include one of these elements without the others!

Data/Warrant/Claim

SUPPLYING WARRANTS AND CLAIMS

Instructions: Complete the following grid by supplying the warrants and claims for the given data. The data in the example was responded to twice to demonstrate how different claims can be drawn from the same data. In other words—there are no right answers!

Example

Data *(the facts)*	Warrant *(reason why you think the data is true or significant)*	Claim *(what—if anything—should be done about the data and the warrant)*
In 2003, a record 46.6% of college-bound seniors earned "A" averages in high school, compared to a record low of 17.6% in 1968.	Teachers are inflating grades for college-bound students.	Teachers should be limited to the number of A's they can award.
In 2003, a record 46.6% of college-bound seniors earned "A" averages in high school, compared to a record low of 17.6% in 1968.	Students now realize the importance of a college education and are working harder to get into good colleges.	Parents and educators should be proud of high-achieving students, but also watch for signs of stress.

Data

In 2003, only 34% of high school seniors reported studying or doing homework 6 or more hours per week; in 1987, 47% of students studied at least 6 hours weekly.

Warrant

_____

_____

_____

_____

_____

Claim

_____

_____

_____

_____

_____

Data

In America, 7 billion gallons of water are used daily on residential lawns.

Warrant

_____

_____

_____

_____

_____

Claim

_____

_____

_____

_____

_____

Data

In 2006, sales of dolls, action figures, and outdoor toys were down sharply, while electronic sales to children were up 16.6%.

Warrant

_____

_____

_____

_____

_____

Claim

_____

_____

_____

_____

_____

Data

Forty-seven percent of dogs in the U.S. are permitted to sleep in a family member's bed.

Warrant

_____

_____

_____

_____

_____

Claim

_____

_____

_____

_____

_____

Data

In 2001, spam accounted for 5% of Internet traffic; today it's often 90%—more than 100 billion unsolicited messages every day.

Warrant

_____

_____

_____

_____

_____

Claim

_____

_____

_____

_____

_____

Data

Nationally, only 46% of people summoned for jury duty actually show up.

Warrant

_____

_____

_____

_____

_____

Claim

_____

_____

_____

_____

_____

Converting the Data/Warrant/Claim to a Paragraph

Example 1: Here is a sample paragraph that uses the warrant (**w**), data (**d**), and claim (**c**) from the first line on the sample grid.

Teachers are guilty of inflating grades for college-bound students (**w**). In 2003, a record 46.6% of college-bound seniors earned A averages in high school, compared with a record low of 17.6% in 1968 (**d**). To avoid this irrational grading, teachers should be limited to the number of As they can award per class (**c**).

Example 2: Here is another sample paragraph that uses the warrant (**w**), data (**d**), and claim (**c**) from the second line on of the sample grid. Note how the same data are used to support a different claim.

Students now realize the importance of a college education and are working harder to get into good colleges (**w**). In 2003, a record 46.6% of college-bound seniors earned A averages in high school, compared with a record low of 17.6% in 1968(**d**). Parents and educators should be proud of high-achieving students, but also watch for signs of stress among these hard-working students (**c**).

Think About It . . .
Why do you suppose the warrant or reason comes before the claim in the paragraph form?

Try It

Select a topic from the grid that appeals to you. Rearrange the information into a paragraph that puts the warrant first, then the data, followed by the claim. Feel free to add additional words or even a sentence or two to make your opinion clear.

CHAPTER 4

Understanding Prompts from the Inside Out

Part of the anxiety clouding the on demand writing experience is that the prompts remain a mystery until the clock starts ticking. While we cannot predict the precise topics addressed by the prompts, we can decipher the expectations of various types of prompts and coach students to recognize these expectations. Does the prompt want me to tell a story? Does it want me to use examples from a selected piece of reading? Does it want me to argue a point? The more comfortable students become with different types of prompts and their formulaic nature, the better they will be able to meet the expectations of the test.

One of the best ways to familiarize students with these expectations is to have them model professionally written prompts as they craft their own prompts for writing. You can place these student-generated prompts in an envelope and draw from it on writing day.

12. The Prompt Generator: Student-Generated Prompts

The best way to dispel an unwarranted fear is to participate in the experience. Afraid of haunted houses? Don a gory mask and jump out from behind a curtain at the next Halloween party. Afraid of the types of questions that might appear on a tough biology final? Try writing a few sample questions. Emulating the prompts that appear on standardized tests can dispel their mystique, make them more familiar, and, therefore, more accessible to student writers.

Why do they need to do this?

The language of the standardized test prompts becomes less mysterious, and the actual topics become more relevant as students work to emulate prompts in their own words. After imitating a series of prompts that begin with the stem "Confirm, challenge, or qualify the following assertion . . . " students begin to recognize an invitation to write a persuasive essay. After the third or fourth attempt at writing a prompt that begins with the stem "Describe a time when . . . " students are able to identify the opportunity to respond with a narrative essay.

Why should they care?

When an essay fails to address a prompt, it qualifies for the lowest score on the rubric. Often well-written, creative essays are assigned to the low end of the scoring scale because they failed to address *all* parts of a prompt or because they told a story when they were expected to construct an argument. Writing prompts allows students to understand the test-maker's intent from the inside out.

How long will this take?

Total time: 55 minutes
   20 minutes to generate prompts
   20 minutes for peer-assessing the prompts' viability
   15 minutes for step 7—an all-important debriefing session

What will you need?

The Prompt Generator (copy for each student)
aphorism journals or copies of a recently studied work of literature

What's the procedure?

1. Announce to students that today they will *not* be writing essays; when the applause dies down, let them know they will be writing essay prompts instead.

2. Ask students to take out their aphorism journals, or you can return their completed Lesson 8 Collecting Aphorisms handout. If you skipped that exercise, don't despair, simply ask students to pull some quoted words from a poster in the room or a recently studied work of literature, essay, or speech.

3. Distribute The Prompt Generator and review. Ask each student to generate 3 prompts—each on a separate scrap of paper. Depending on which tests are looming on the horizon, you can ask students to generate all three types of prompts or just the one that applies to their upcoming on demand writing challenge.

4. Tell students to write their names on the back of their papers to preserve anonymity as the prompts are later passed around the room for peer review. If you anticipate problems with peeking, ask students to use their student identification number or the last four digits of their home phone number.

5. You can then conduct a brief read-around as students pass their papers within a group or up and down a row, with the readers indicating one of the following marks on the front of the prompt:

    "+" for an outstandingly creative and clearly worded prompt

    "√" for a serviceable clear prompt

    "–" for a prompt that is not clearly worded

6. You will have to enforce the "no peeking at the back of the paper" rule so the prompts are judged on their quality not their authorship.

7. Debrief with students about the common qualities shared among the top-ranked prompts. This discussion is an invaluable part of the lesson and will get them even closer to understanding a prompt from the inside out.

Lesson extensions

- You can give extra credit to the prompts receiving the greatest number of "+" marks.
- You can add the prompts with the greater number of "+" marks to a classroom's cache of prompts that can be accessed for future on demand writing practice.

The Prompt Generator

I. To Generate a Prompt Worthy of the SAT I . . .

1. On a half sheet of paper, copy an aphorism from your aphorism journal or copy a quotation from something we've read in class or even from an inspirational poster in the classroom.

2. Choose one of the following set of directions and copy it below your quotation:
   - Plan and write an essay in which you confirm, challenge, or qualify the above assertion. Support your position with reasons and examples from your reading, studies, experiences, or observations.
   - Citing examples from your reading, observations, and experiences, agree or disagree with the ideas expressed in the above quotation.

Sample SAT Prompt (from www.collegeboard.com)

Quotation: "A society composed of men and women who are not bound by convention—in other words, they do not act according to what others say or do—is far more lively than one in which all people behave alike. When each person's character is developed individually and differences of opinion are acceptable, it is beneficial to interact with new people because they are not mere replicas of those whom one has already met."

Adapted from Bertrand Russell, *The Conquest of Happiness*

Prompt: Is it better for a society when people act as individuals rather than copying the ideas and opinions of others? Plan and write an essay in which you develop your point of view on this issue. Support your position with reasoning and examples taken from your reading, studies, experience, or observations.

Congratulations! You have just generated an SAT prompt. Write your name on the back of the paper only.

II. To Generate a Prompt Worthy of the ACT Writing Exam . . .

1. On a separate piece of paper, describe an issue relevant to high school students (e.g., drivers' licenses, work permits, curfew, etc.).

2. Briefly provide two different perspectives on the issue.
3. Conclude the prompt by asking, "In your opinion, should . . . ?"
4. Include these directions after your question:
   - In your essay, take a position on this question. You may write about either one of the two points of view given, or you may present a different point of view on this question. Use specific reasons and examples to support your position.

Sample ACT Prompt (from www.actstudent.org)

Issue: Educators debate extending high school to five years because of increasing demands on students from employers and colleges to participate in extracurricular activities and community service in addition to having high grades. Some educators support extending high school to five years because they think students need more time to achieve all that is expected of them. Other educators do not support extending high school to five years because they think students would lose interest in school and attendance would drop in the fifth year. In your opinion, should high school be extended to five years?

Prompt: In your essay, take a position on this question. You may write about either one of the two points of view given, or you may present a different point of view on this question. Use specific reasons and examples to support your position.

Congratulations! You have just generated an ACT prompt. Write the entire prompt on a separate piece of paper. Place your name on the back of the paper only.

Think About It . . .
Which is easier to construct, an SAT I prompt or an ACT prompt? Why?
Which seems easier to respond to as a writer? Why?

III. To Generate a Prompt Worthy of a College Placement Exam . . .

Many junior colleges and state universities insist that incoming freshmen sit for a placement exam that usually consists of a series of multiple-choice questions on grammar and mechanics and an essay prompt that mirrors that of the SAT I or that invites students to write an autobiographical narrative. The subject of the prompt must be nondiscriminatory and cannot presuppose knowledge. For instance, the prompts are not permitted to ask the writer to reveal his or her religious beliefs nor are they to expect them to have knowledge of a particular issue like current gas prices.

1. Begin by making a list of experiences that most humans encounter (e.g., making a wish that doesn't come true, encountering a roadblock to success, misunderstanding a friend, worrying unnecessarily, etc.).

2. Choose one of the experiences and plug it into the formula:
   Describe a time when you _____.
   Vividly recreate the incident with detailed description and conclude by assessing what you learned from the experience.

Sample College-Placement Prompt from a Local Junior College
(from www.santarosa.edu/app/placement):
Before you begin writing, consider the topic carefully and plan what you will say. Your essay should be as well organized and as carefully written as you can make it. Be sure to use specific examples to support your ideas.

Most people have read a book or seen a play, movie, or television program that affected their feelings or behavior in some important way. Discuss such an experience of your own. Describe the book, play, movie, or television program and explain why you regard its effect on you as important.

Congratulations! You have just generated a college-placement prompt. Write the entire prompt on a separate piece of scrap paper. Place your name on the back of the paper only.

13. The Qualified Thesis for Waffle-Lovers: Generating Thesis Statements That Acknowledge an Opposition

Many on demand writing prompts give students the options of confirming, challenging, or qualifying a statement. Often student writers argue that they can't support just one side or the other. On the debate team, students must be able to uphold opposing sides of the same argument. One round they will be assigned the affirmative position and the next round the negative position on the same issue. Most beginners have a difficult time with this until they realize they have to find something—anything—they can uphold on one side or the other. Finding the foothold of an argument on one side of the issue often leads to strengthening their position on the other side. Debaters are also forced to depersonalize their arguments, approaching arguments as exercises in strategies rather than revelations of their personal beliefs. The more students are encouraged to treat their essays as exercises in reasoning and structure—more like a math problem than a diary or journal entry—the less likely they will waffle.

To ensure that wafflers develop a point of view in their essays, I encourage them to "qualify" the claim by writing a qualified thesis. Qualified claims save time and set parameters for the writer of an argument. To illustrate, here is the sample SAT I writing prompt from The College Board Web site:

> Are people motivated to achieve by personal satisfaction rather than by money or fame? Plan and write an essay in which you develop your point of view on this issue. Support your position with reasoning and examples taken from your reading, studies, experience, or observations.

A sample waffle-lover thesis might read, "Both money and personal satisfaction motivate people; it's hard to say that one is more important than the other." A sample qualified thesis would read, "Although money may initially motivate people, tending the fires of personal satisfaction keeps them achieving even when they've earned enough money to survive." This former waffler now has a position and structure. The writer can first address how people are initially motivated by money, then transition into why fame remains the perpetual generator of achievement.

To aid students in generating a qualified thesis, work to develop a series of questions to help them arrive at their qualified position. Here's an example from a midterm prompt that followed students studying Shakespeare's *Macbeth* and Machiavelli's *The Prince*:

Prompt: Citing examples from our readings, your observations, and experiences, determine to what extent effective leaders can remain true to themselves.

Questions to guide students toward a qualified thesis:

      What should an effective leader be willing to compromise?

      What should an effective leader never compromise?

Qualified thesis generator:

After answering the above questions, fill in the blanks:

      Although effective leaders may have to compromise

      _____ (strive to list only one quality),

      they should never compromise

      _____ (list one to three qualities).

While these questions and the qualified thesis generator are specific to the midterm prompt, it is possible to acquaint students with a series of general questions that can help them extract a qualified thesis from the generic standardized prompts. In debate case construction, this procedure is often referred to as the "harms/benefits analysis."

Why do they need to do this?

Even the lowest passing score on a standardized rubric demands that the writer "upholds a consistent point of view." Students who are ambivalent on their position are served best by qualifying a claim rather than admitting their uncertainty—which can lead to failure.

Why should they care?

A qualified position gives students two bangs for their buck—a clear position and structure for their essay.

How long will this take?

Total time: 60–70 minutes

 30 minutes to generate qualified theses

 20–30 minutes to roadmap the qualified response

 10 minutes if you choose to peer-assess the roadmaps

What will you need?

The Qualified Thesis Generator (copy for each student)

Qualified Roadmapping (copy for each student).

Qualified Roadmapping Rubric (optional: 2 copies for each student)

What's the procedure?

1. Begin by emphasizing (perhaps with a copy of the SAT I scoring rubric found in Appendix 2) that to receive a passing score on a timed essay, it *must* develop a clear point of view.

    > ✎ **Peter Prickly:** Then how come lots of the prompt instructions tell us that we can qualify our response. Doesn't that mean we can argue both sides?
    > **Mrs. Snippy:** No. It means you can acknowledge a valid argument from the other side, but you are still obligated to uphold a clear position.

2. Illustrate, using sample prompts, that the instructions often invite writers to qualify their responses.

    For instance in the directions to the ACT essay prompt, students will be told:
    > "In your essay, take a position on this question. You may write about either one of the two points of view given, or you may present a different point of view on this question."

    In the directions to the free response essay question on the AP Language and Composition essay, students are frequently told to:
    > "Plan and write an essay in which you confirm, challenge, or qualify the above assertion."

3. Illustrate for students how a qualified position gives strength to an argument as well as providing structure using the following example:

Let's say Peter is arguing with his father about staying out late on Friday night. He could say:
> "Dad, I am responsible—I won't do anything stupid."

If he's smart, however, he'll qualify his argument:
> "Dad, I know you're worried about me doing something stupid, but you've taught me to be responsible, and I've been waiting for this opportunity to show you."

Peter has not only addressed his Dad's argument about responsibility, but if his Dad is still reluctant to say "yes," Peter has provided a structure for the rest of his argument. He could then provide examples of how he was taught responsibility and follow those with the claim that Friday night would provide an excellent opportunity to prove his responsibility.

4. Distribute The Qualified Thesis Generator and clarify the directions for students, instructing them to first answer the short questions under each of the prompts and then fill in the blanks on the qualified thesis generator.

5. After 30 minutes, students should have had a chance to individually respond to the questions under the first 2 prompts. Invite them to share their qualified theses aloud. Answers will vary considerably.

6. Distribute Qualified Roadmapping. Take 10 minutes to read over and discuss the sample roadmap, emphasizing how the thesis and roadmap both acknowledge an opposition while developing a clear position.

7. Direct students to follow Steps 2 and 3, which ask them to roadmap one of the qualified theses that they just generated in the previous exercise. This should take about 20 minutes.

8. You can collect the Qualified Roadmapping sheets and assess them using the Qualified Roadmapping Rubric, or you can ask students to swap roadmaps with a partner and peer-assess each other's work using the rubric.

> **Hint:** Before assessing the student roadmaps, I like to acquaint students with the scoring rubric by asking them to informally use it to assess the sample qualified roadmap.

I then collect the roadmaps and staple two Roadmapping Rubrics to each one before I redistribute the roadmaps to random students in the class. After each student has had a chance to read and assess a roadmap, I then re-collect the papers and average the two scores. This compensates for overly generous graders and the sticklers, leaving most papers with at least a B average, yet still imparting a sense of scrutiny to the students that extends beyond merely awarding credit for filling the page.

The Qualified Thesis Generator

Instructions: Answer the series of questions under each prompt before proceeding to the qualified thesis generator.

PROMPT 1: EXTENDING HIGH SCHOOL

In your opinion, should high school be extended to five years? Plan and write an essay in which support your opinion with reasons and examples from your reading, studies, experiences, or observations.

What would be the benefits of extending high school to five years?

_____

_____

_____

What would be the harms of extending high school to five years?

_____

_____

_____

Have you listed more benefits or harms?

_____

_____

_____

Qualified Thesis Generator
If you listed more harms plug into the following qualified thesis generator:

Although extending high school to five years would (list one benefit) _____

_____, it would (list 1–2 harms)

_____.

If you listed more benefits, plug into the following qualified thesis generator:

Although extending high school to five years would (list 1 harm) _____
_____, it would (list 1–2 benefits)
_____.

Sample Qualified Thesis: Although extending high school to five years would require an increase in funding and possibly state taxes, it would save us money in the long run by requiring less college remediation and providing a more capable work force.

PROMPT 2: FEAR VS. LOVE

"It is better to be feared than loved." Plan and write an essay in which you confirm, challenge, or qualify the above assertion. Support your position with reasons and examples from your reading, studies, experiences, or observations.

List examples where it is better to be feared than loved:

_____
_____
_____

List examples where it is better to be loved than feared:

_____
_____
_____

Qualified Thesis Generator
If you had more examples of being feared, plug into this thesis generator:

Although (mention an instance where being loved is more important than being feared)
_____, being feared is preferable to
being loved in situations such as (list 1–2 instances where being feared is preferred)
_____.

If you had more examples of being loved, plug into this thesis generator:

Although (mention an instance where being feared is more important than being loved) _____, being loved is preferable to being feared in situations such as (list 1–2 instances where being loved is preferred)

_____.

Sample Qualified Thesis: Although it may be better for a care provider like a mother or father to be loved rather than feared, it is preferable for managers of large groups to be feared rather than loved to instill a sense of justice in the group.

Think About It . . .
Why do you provide an imbalance of harms to benefits in your thesis? How does this avoid sounding like you are waffling?

Qualified Roadmapping

STEP 1: Read over the sample qualified thesis and roadmap. Notice how the first supporting argument in the roadmap acknowledges the opposition.

Sample Qualified Thesis and Roadmap:

Thesis: Although extending high school to five years would require an increase in funding and possibly state taxes, it would save us money in the long run by requiring less college remediation and providing a more capable work force.

Supporting Reasons—why the thesis is correct:

1. **Supporting reason—acknowledges the opposition:** Extending high school to five years would cost more.

    Example(s):

    More funding would be necessary to support additional teachers and materials.

    State taxes would probably have to be increased temporarily to generate the necessary revenue.

2. **Supporting reason—addresses the position:** Increasing high school to five years would save the state money on college remediation.

    Example(s):

    Currently ill-prepared college students tax the system by requiring remedial courses that are taught by overqualified professors and graduate students.

    If students' college-readiness was addressed in high school, it would cost the state less because high school instructors are paid less than professors.

3. **Supporting reason—addresses the position:** In the long run, the state would save money with a better-prepared workforce.

    Example(s):

    Workers who are better educated require less training and can begin making meaningful contributions to society sooner.

    Workers who are ill-prepared in basic math and communication skills grow frustrated and are more likely to be fired.

Conclusion—answers the question, "Therefore what?":
Spending the extra money now to thoroughly educate high school students will benefit the state financially in the long run and benefit the students for a lifetime.

Step 2: Jot down one of the thesis statements you generated with the qualified thesis generator (remember to lead off with one of the following "Although . . . ", "Despite the fact that . . . ", or "Even though . . . "):

Thesis:

_____

_____

Step 3: Roadmap your supporting arguments.

Supporting Reasons—why the thesis is correct:

1. **Supporting reason—acknowledges the opposition:**
    example(s):

    _____

    _____

2. **Supporting reason—addresses the position:**
    example(s):

    _____

    _____

3. **Supporting reason—addresses the position:**
    example(s):

    _____

    _____

Conclusion—answers the question, "Therefore what?":

_____

_____

Qualified Roadmapping Rubric

Name: _____

Topic: _____

	Score
Preparation (completed template)	
Prompt development (reasons and proof clearly connect to the language of the prompt)	
Proof (specific references to information from the news article)	
Position (acknowledges the opposition, yet maintains a clear position)	
Total	/20

Scoring
5-Exceptional! **4**-Accomplished **3**-Competent **2**-Incomplete **1**-Missing

14. Focusing a Vague Prompt: Qualified Criterion-Based Thesis Statements (yes, that's a mouthful)

In debate, teams usually present a case built around a criterion—a means of measuring the validity of their arguments. For instance, given the prompt, "Is it better to be feared or loved?," one team might select a criterion of justice and argue that being feared is preferable to being loved in matters of justice. They might cite how teachers and courtroom judges will be able to demonstrate a greater sense of fairness if they are feared rather than loved. Using that same criterion of justice, the other side could counter that fear implies mistrust and that the perpetrator of fear must be acting capriciously, which is a far cry from the evenhanded justice being demonstrated. The argument volley would continue, but what's worth noting is the focus that the criterion of justice has given an otherwise tremendously broad topic.

Similarly, if Peter Prickly's criterion for measuring the worth of Mrs. Snippy's class is its speed, and Mrs. Snippy's criterion is depth, their argument would sound something like this:

> 🖋 **Peter Prickly:** I don't like this class. It moves too slowly.
>
> **Mrs. Snippy:** Perhaps you need to consider things more deeply rather than so quickly.

Why do they need to do this?
Students still struggling with qualifying a thesis may not be up for the challenge of adding a criterion to the mix, but those who are up for the challenge will find that their essays maintain a tighter focus.

Why should they care?
Standardized essay prompts are often intentionally vague and value-based in an attempt to avoid privileging previous knowledge. A criterion-based position helps students focus their response in an on demand writing situation and avoid the amorphous blob that ensues when a writer tries to cover all possibilities in a short time.

How long will this take?

Total time: 50 minutes

    20 minutes to introduce the concept of a criterion and to demonstrate how/why it is used

    20 minutes to generate a criterion-based qualified thesis

    10 minutes to share aloud the sample theses

What will you need?

The Criterion-Based Qualified Thesis Generator (copy for each student)

What's the procedure?

1. Begin by getting student comfortable with the term "criterion."

    🔎 **Hints:**

    - You could ask students to list the characteristics of a good friend. Then explain that those qualities are their criteria. If they could choose only one essential quality to measure the worth of a good friend—that would be their number 1 criterion.

    - I like to introduce the concept of a criterion by citing an example with which students are very familiar—dating. I begin by telling them the story of my friend John, who confided in me that he was struggling to find a girl who met all of his criteria: beautiful, fun, and shorter than he. When I told John that he needed to stop being so picky, I insisted that he select just one quality he was looking for in a girlfriend. He said, "Short." I then tell the class that John now has a criterion—a way of measuring whether someone is potential girlfriend material. In an argument, a criterion helps you measure to what extent you're meeting your standard.

2. Tell students that they will be revisiting what they learned about qualifying a thesis and adding a criterion to make their thesis statements even stronger.

3. Distribute The Criterion-Based Qualified Thesis Generator. Review and allow 20 minutes for students to maneuver their way through the thesis generator.

4. Encourage the class to share aloud their final thesis statements and, as they do, call on other students to identify the criterion that is being used in the thesis.

Emphasize that the criterion is another variable that helps to distinguish one position from another, thus improving the clarity of a writer's position—a reasonable goal for any rubric.

Lesson extensions

- Ask students to roadmap an essay based on the criterion-based qualified thesis statement they crafted for the exercise.
- Give students another value-based prompt, such as "Is trust or kindness more important in a relationship?" or "Is peace or progress more important to a nation?" and let them generate their own criterion-based qualified thesis statement without the hand-holding of the thesis generator questions.
- If students successfully maneuver their way through the criterion-based thesis generator, you could insist that they generate this type of thesis on their next essay. The next challenge will be making sure they maintain the focus dictated by the criterion.

The Criterion-Based Qualified Thesis Generator

Instructions: Answer the questions that arise from the following prompt.

PROMPT: "Actions speak louder than words." Plan and write an essay in which you confirm, challenge, or qualify the above assertion. Support your position with reasons and examples from your reading, studies, experiences, or observations.

1. List examples where actions speak louder than words:

   _____

   _____

   _____

2. List examples where words had more impact than actions:

   _____

   _____

   _____

3. What seems to be your means of measuring whether words or actions speak louder? Lasting impact? Efficiency? Swiftness? Other? Identify your criterion.

   _____

   _____

   _____

If you listed more examples under question 1 (actions speak louder) than question 2, plug into this thesis generator:

Despite the fact that (list 1 example of words having impact)

_____, actions speak louder because they are more (identify your criterion from above)

_____.

If you listed more examples under question 2 (words speak louder), plug into this thesis generator:

Despite the fact that (list 1 example of actions having impact)

_____, words speak louder because they are more (identify your criterion from above)

_____.

Think About It . . .
How does a criterion in a thesis offer the rest of the essay a tighter focus?

CHAPTER 5

Fleshing Out the Essay

Up until this point students have practiced brainstorming topics, mapping out responses, and even generating carefully crafted thesis statements. But when the stopwatch is racing, the bulk of the students' time will be spent paragraphing the essay.

What follows is a series of exercises to assist students in fleshing out their skeletal outlines to the prompts. In addition to being reminded to develop muscular body paragraphs, students will need to be coached on slimming down their introductions and conclusions.

In traditional writing practices—those that involve multiple drafts—students have been trained to write extensive introductions and bulky summarizing conclusions. In on demand writing situations, however, students simply will not have time to craft intricate and creative introductions and conclusions, and, most important—while the evaluators still appreciate a good first impression and a sense of closure, none of the rubrics reward essays for catchy introductions or magnificent conclusions.

15. Lean Mean Introductions: How to Write Skimpy Introductions That Pack a Punch

While plunging into the opening paragraph of an essay with nothing more than a well-crafted thesis statement would not be grounds for failure, most evaluators expect an essay to have an introductory sentence.

Students are traditionally taught to begin an essay with a story or personal anecdote that draws the reader into their topic. Many of the best students—those who have traditionally performed well in English language arts—will write introductory paragraphs that cover nearly three-quarters of a page. Many of these students find themselves only halfway through their first body paragraph at the end of their first practice timed-write. They have a hard time knowing how to begin without a hearty first paragraph.

Coaching students to whip out brief but compelling introductory statements can satisfy both the expectation for an introduction as well as saving time that can be more valuably spent crafting body paragraphs and a meaningful conclusion.

Why do they need to do this?
Essays are expected to have introductions. On demand writing situations require that a limited amount of time and ink be spent on introductions. These exercises will wean students away from previous coaching that an introduction needs to elaborate on the topic and gradually funnel down to the thesis. Once students practice the knack of "grab and go" introductions, they'll come to rely on their efficiency.

Why should they care?
Crafting an effective introduction is important, but it can soak up valuable time that almost certainly is better spent developing the thesis in the body paragraphs and in drawing a meaningful conclusion. Knowing that several instant introduction generators are available lessens the frustration of starting a timed essay.

How long will this take?
Total time: 35–50 minutes
   5 minutes to roadmap a response to a prompt
   30 minutes to complete the student handout without interruption
   15 minutes if you opt to pause and read aloud sample introductions with the students

What will you need?

Lean Mean Introductions (copy for each student)

an essay prompt

What's the procedure?

1. Ask your students about how they have been coached to begin an essay. Most will respond that they've been taught to begin with a paragraph that introduces the topic followed by a thesis statement.

2. Reassure students that traditional introductory paragraphs are fine if they are given unlimited time to work on the essay, but, with a timed essay, they need new strategy for essay introductions.

3. Announce an essay prompt and give the students 5 minutes to craft a thesis statement—preferably qualified—in response. NOTE: You can skip steps 3 and 4 if you prefer to recycle qualified thesis statements from previous exercises.

4. Distribute Lean Mean Introductions. Read aloud the sample prompt and sample thesis on the handout so the students are familiar with the topic used in the sample introductions that follow.

5. Ask students to copy their prompt and thesis statement in the space provided.

6. Read aloud the first sample introductory sentence—The Rhetorical Question. Point out that the sentence does more than repeat the prompt in the form of a question. Ask students to write a rhetorical question they could use to introduce their thesis.

7. Review the worksheet so students become familiar with the sample introductory sentences they will be using as a template.

8. Tell students to complete the rest of the worksheet or proceed box by box. In total, completing the worksheet should take approximately 30 minutes.

> 🔎 **Hint:** It's very helpful to pause to read aloud a few sample introductory sentences as the students generate them. This will reassure students that an unlimited number of possible "right" answers are available and expose them to some great brief introductions.

9. In the final box on the worksheet, ask students to select their favorite sample introduction and copy it, then follow with its thesis statement.

10. Then ask them to select their favorite introductory sentence—you may want to direct them to consider which introductory sentence connects best to their thesis.

11. Collect the handouts and save for the next lesson on paragraphing.

Lesson extensions

- Allow students to consult the Lean Mean Introductions sheet the next time you ask them to write an essay.
- Conduct some timed drills where you give students a prompt and a total of 5 minutes to roadmap, craft a thesis, and write an introductory sentence.

Lean Mean Introductions

With limited time to write an essay, you don't have the luxury of crafting lengthy introductions. The following exercise will demonstrate how to "skimpify" your introductions to only a sentence followed by a thesis without lessening their impact on the reader.

Instructions:

1. Jot down the prompt your teacher gives you.
2. Note the sample thesis given in response to the sample prompt.
3. Take 5 minutes to craft a thesis—preferably qualified—in response to your prompt. Write it in the space provided below.

Sample prompt	Your prompt
School start time should be extended until 9 a.m. for all public high schools. Plan and write an essay in which you confirm, challenge, or qualify the above assertion. Support your position with reasons and examples from your reading, studies, experiences, or observations.	

Sample thesis	Your thesis
Although extending school start time would lengthen the school day, the time spent in class would be more educationally valuable if classes didn't begin until 9 a.m.	

4. Experiment with writing different types of introductory sentences for your thesis. A sample is provided next to a space for you to write your own. (The space is limited as a reminder to keep your introductions brief!)

The Rhetorical Question:
Asking a Question That Leads to Your Position

Sample intro	Your intro
If most employers expect their workers to report for work by 9 a.m., why do we expect teenagers to be at their desks ready to work as early as 7:45 am?	

Dine with the Opposition:
Acknowledge and Refute an Opposing Argument

Sample intro	Your intro
Nobody will be thrilled to have the school bell ring later at dismissal, but everyone will be glad when the alarm doesn't ring before dawn to begin another school day.	

The Sensational Detail or Startling Fact:
Shock Your Reader into Paying Attention

Sample intro with sensational detail	Your intro
The students who nod off during early-morning classes are most likely not dreaming of their lessons.	

Sample intro with a fact	
Studies show that one of three American teens don't get enough sleep.	

The Quotation:
Use Someone Else's Words to Launch Your Position

Sample intro	Your intro
"The early bird gets the worm," but I doubt he could get calculus at 7:45 a.m.	

The Analogy:
Compare Your Topic with Something Else

Sample intro	Your intro
You don't schedule classes at 7:45 a.m. for the same reason that you don't schedule open heart surgeries for 11:00 p.m. If you're after optimum results, students, like surgeons, need to be well-rested.	

The Literary Allusion:
Reference Literature You've Studied

Sample intro	Your intro
Throughout literature, toiling into the wee hours is reserved for deviants like Dr. Frankenstein and Macbeth.	

5. Select your favorite introduction, rewrite it, and attach your thesis to it.

Take Your Pick!

Select your favorite sample introductory sentence and write it below. Write the thesis at the end.	Select your favorite introductory sentence and rewrite it below. Write your thesis at the end.

Look at that! You've crafted a complete introductory paragraph using only two sentences. Let this be your goal in future timed essays.

Think About It . . .

Why would a compelling story be a good way to begin an essay being written at home, but a dangerous way to start a 25-minute timed essay?

16. Body Paragraphs That Don't Stand Alone: How to Craft Body Paragraphs That Develop a Thesis

Body paragraphs should begin with claims that reconnect to the thesis. Even a rapid-fire reader will be able to notice the supporting arguments clearly this way and see that they really add up.

Ending body paragraphs with an answer to the question "Therefore what?" assures an internal conclusion, which can be very helpful if time robs the writer of composing a thorough concluding paragraph. The response to the question "Therefore what?" also forces the writer to reconnect to his thesis, thus ensuring focus.

Framing a body paragraph with a claim and an internally drawn conclusion develops the thesis—provided, of course, that the middle of the paragraph is chock-full of specific supporting detail and meaningful commentary.

Why do they need to do this?
Beginning body paragraphs with claims rather than facts or observations ensures that the thesis is being supported and developed. Ending body paragraphs with internally drawn conclusions also ensures thesis development and indicates critical thinking—two basic expectations of any standardized rubric.

Why should they care?
These exercises in body paragraph structure give students a framework that is easy to plug into but also meaningful. It may be formulaic, but it's a formula that leads to logical development of an argument or idea.

How long will this take?
Total time: 35–55 minutes
  15 minutes to read aloud page 1 of the student handout and to answer questions
  20 minutes to complete page 2 of the student handout
  20 minutes to complete and correct the optional exercise Laying Claim to Your Topic Sentences

What will you need?

Body Paragraphs That Don't Stand Alone (copy for each student)

The thesis statements written in the previous lesson, "Lean Mean Introductions" or thesis statements generated by a new prompt

Laying Claim to Your Topic Sentences (copy for each student) optional

What's the procedure?

1. Begin by reviewing with students the meaning of the word "claim" as used in Lesson 11. Emphasize that a claim is an argument, distinguishable from fact or observation.

2. If students require additional assistance in clarifying this distinction, distribute and ask the students to complete Laying Claim to Your Topic Sentences. This exercise will take about 20 minutes for the students to complete and correct.

> *Hint:* In helping my students distinguish between a claim and an observation, I ask them to imagine two cantankerous old men sitting on a front porch. If one states a claim, the other will surely counter:
>
> "I think it's going to be a dry winter."
> "Nope. By the looks of those clouds, storm's a-brewin'."
> "Those aren't rain clouds."
>
> Presumably this argument could last all afternoon.
> However, if one man states an observation, all the other can do is agree and the conversation ends.
>
> "It's raining."
> "Yep."
>
> I tell my students that their goal is to keep the argument alive.

3. Distribute Body Paragraphs That Don't Stand Alone.

4. Read aloud the sample thesis statement and its corresponding body paragraphs, pausing to discuss how each body paragraph begins with a claim that is a debatable statement and how each paragraph ends with an internally drawn conclusion that answers the question "Therefore what?"

5. Direct their attention to the *Think About It . . .* question and encourage several students to weigh in with why the claim is reserved for the topic sentence of the paragraph.

6. Distribute the students' thesis statements from the previous lesson, Lean Mean Introductions, or distribute a new prompt and ask them to craft a thesis statement.

7. Direct students to page 2 of the student handout and ask them to jot down their thesis statement in the space provided.

8. Ask students to fill in the material requested for body paragraphs 1 and 2, pausing to answer the questions in brackets.

9. Collect the students' work and set it aside for use in the next lesson.

Lesson extensions

- As students work to complete the two body paragraphs, you may want to engage in an informal peer review of claims by directing students to ask a partner to check whether their claims are, in fact, debatable statements.

- You may want to conduct timed drills in which you give students 10 minutes to craft a thesis and single body paragraph in response to a prompt.

- As added practice in helping students distinguish observations from claims, distribute Laying Claim to Your Topic Sentences.

Body Paragraphs That Don't Stand Alone

Instructions:

1. Read the sample thesis statement below and its corresponding body paragraphs. Note how each body paragraph begins with a claim that is a debatable statement and how each paragraph ends with an internally drawn conclusion that answers the question, "Therefore what?"

2. At the top of page 2, jot down your thesis statement from Lean Mean Introductions or craft a thesis statement from the new prompt your teacher gave you.

3. Fill in the material requested for body paragraphs one and two, pausing to answer the questions in brackets.

Sample

THESIS: Although extending school start time would lengthen the school day, the time spent in class would be more educationally valuable if classes didn't begin until 9 a.m.

BODY PARAGRAPH 1

Sample claim: The benefits of starting the school day later outweigh any harms of ending the day later. *[Is this a debatable statement? Yes. One could argue that the harms outweigh the benefits]*. Although, ending the school day later may be problematic for older students who work or for athletes who may have to miss part of their last class of the day, this would only affect a small portion of the students. Whereas a later start time benefits all of the students with much needed rest—and even the teachers who may have been up late the night before chaperoning that basketball game. *[Therefore what?]* The inconvenience to and impact on a few students who bag groceries or play badminton are minor compared with the healthy effect of a full night's rest on a brain expected to both be awake and to perform at its best.

BODY PARAGRAPH 2

Sample claim: Students and teachers who have had the recommended 8–9 hours of sleep perform better than those who are sleep-deprived and relying on caffeine to keep their chins from hitting their chests. *[Is this a debatable statement? Yes. One could argue that currently students and teachers manage to stay awake and perform.]* Studies have shown that the teenage brain is hardwired to stay awake late at night and to come to consciousness after sunrise. Just because students must wake early doesn't mean they were able to go to bed early, resulting in sleep-deprived brains that function below capacity in academically demanding classes like trigonometry or biology that could make or break a student's future. ***[Therefore what?]*** Extra sleep translates into extra learning.

Think About It . . .
Why are the middle sentences of the body paragraphs not necessarily claims or arguments?

Your Turn!

1. Transcribe your prompt.

Prompt:

_____

_____

_____

2. Jot down your thesis statement.

Thesis:

_____

_____

_____

3. Fill in the material requested for body paragraphs one and two, pausing to answer the questions in the brackets.

BODY PARAGRAPH 1
Claim:

_____

_____

[Is this a debatable statement? _____ If so, how so?

_____*]*.

At Least Two Sentences of Support for the Claim:

_____

_____

_____

Therefore what?

_____

_____

_____

Body Paragraph 2

Claim:

_____

_____

[Is this a debatable statement? _____ If so, how so?

_____ *].*

At Least Two Sentences of Support for the Claim:

_____

_____

_____

_____

Therefore what?

_____

_____

_____

Laying Claim to Your Topic Sentences

By now, you've heard that body paragraphs are best if begun with a claim rather than an observation.

An **observation** is a fact or statement that can't be argued
(e.g., We write timed essays in our English class.).
A **claim** is an assertion that can be disputed
(e.g., Writing timed essays is fun!).

Instructions: Place a **C** in the space below if the statement is a claim or an **O** if the statement is an observation.

____ **1.** Writing timed essays prepares us for college.

____ **2.** My cousin Peter had to write timed essays in all of his college classes.

____ **3.** My dad even had to write a timed memo as part of a job interview.

____ **4.** Writing well under time constraints has benefits that extend beyond college.

____ **5.** Being able to organize your thoughts quickly is important in on demand writing.

____ **6.** Most scoring rubrics allow for misspelled words.

____ **7.** What matters most in a timed essay are specific supporting details.

____ **8.** My teacher says to always title your timed essays.

____ **9.** Timed essays do not necessarily have 5 paragraphs.

____ **10.** Lengthy introductions are unnecessary in a timed essay.

____ **11.** Some students write their introductions last.

____ **12.** A good thesis addresses all parts of a writing prompt.

____ **13.** A good conclusion does more than summarize the points of the essay.

____ **14.** A conclusion is the last paragraph of an essay.

____ **15.** A conclusion should draw from the evidence presented in the essay.

____ **16.** Many people fear running out of time before reaching a conclusion.

____ **17.** Pacing is an important part of writing a timed essay.

____ **18.** Many people improve their timed essay strategies but still hate writing essays.

____ **19.** Some people prefer to write timed essays rather than multiple-draft papers.

____ **20.** The more timed essays you write, the more fun they become!

Laying Claim to Your Topic Sentences Answer Key

C **1.** Writing timed essays prepares us for college.

O **2.** My cousin Peter had to write timed essays in all of his college classes.

O **3.** My dad even had to write a timed memo as part of a job interview.

C **4.** Writing well under time constraints has benefits that extend beyond college.

C **5.** Being able to organize your thoughts quickly is important in on demand writing.

O **6.** Most scoring rubrics allow for misspelled words.

C **7.** What matters most in a timed essay are specific supporting details.

O **8.** My teacher says to always title your timed essays.

C **9.** Timed essays do not necessarily have 5 paragraphs.

C **10.** Lengthy introductions are unnecessary in a timed essay.

O **11.** Some students write their introductions last.

C **12.** A good thesis addresses all parts of a writing prompt.

C **13.** A good conclusion does more than summarize the points of the essay.

O **14.** A conclusion is the last paragraph of an essay.

C **15.** A conclusion should draw from the evidence presented in the essay.

O **16.** Many people fear running out of time before reaching a conclusion.

C **17.** Pacing is an important part of writing a timed essay.

O **18.** Many people improve their timed essay strategies but still hate writing essays.

O **19.** Some people prefer to write timed essays rather than multiple-draft papers.

C **20.** The more timed essays you write, the more fun they become!

17. So What?: How to Write Meaningful Conclusions

Students may have been taught a method of ending an essay that is not useful in a timed situation, e.g., the lengthy introductions that they have been encouraged to construct for multiple-draft essays.

Two of the most common conclusion strategies are highly ineffective for timed essays. The first is to summarize previous points, or "tell 'em what you told 'em." Not only does this strategy fail to draw a conclusion, it is unnecessary in such a brief essay. In a timed essay, the writer is lucky to have made 2 or 3 claims; an adept evaluator doesn't need a review of these points when she can simply glance at the page and see them for herself. A 10-page term paper may benefit from a summary of the major ideas; a 3-paragraph essay doesn't.

The second strategy commonly taught to students who have been coached on the 5-paragraph essay structure is to reiterate the thesis statement. However, beginning and ending with the same statement creates a circle, not an essay.

In fairness to the teachers who have done a fantastic job of preparing my students for the rigors of writing in high school, I am careful not to debunk what the students have been taught. I explain why these methods may be effective for longer pieces of writing or for first-time experiments with full-length essay writing but that a new strategy needs to be employed for the demands of timed writing. I call this the "So what?" strategy.

Why do they need to do this?

A meaningful conclusion is an essential part of an essay. An essay that trails off or simply circles back to the original thesis lacks critical thinking and may seem unfinished—because it is! Since one of the goals of an on demand writing task is to measure whether the student can complete an essay in the allotted time, a solid conclusion may be the writer's best shot at proving this beyond a doubt.

Why should they care?

The last element an evaluator reads before scoring an essay is the conclusion. It stands to reason that those final words should be meaningful and cogent, not merely a rehash. Rehearsing a few simple questions that can be asked and answered—literally in a matter of seconds—is worth the time and trouble if it means compelling the reader to consider the impact of the points discussed throughout the essay.

How long will this take?

Total time: 35–47 minutes

- 5–7 minutes to discuss previously taught conclusion strategies
- 10 minutes to review the sample conclusions and to discuss effectiveness
- 20 minutes to write 4 different types of conclusions
- 10 minutes for an optional read-around of student work

What will you need?

completed Body Paragraphs That Don't Stand Alone handout from Lesson 16
So What? (copy for each student)

What's the procedure?

1. Begin by leading a brief class discussion on the topic: "How have you been taught to end an essay?" You may want to note the students' replies on the board.

2. Collect as many strategies as possible before you explain that an on demand writing situation limits the writer's ability to adhere to traditional strategies.

> 🔍 **Hint:** In your discussion of previously taught conclusion strategies, take great pains to emphasize the ineffectiveness of simply reiterating the original thesis statement—a method most students have been taught. I illustrate the ineffectiveness of this method by drawing a circle on the board from a fixed point. I then state, "If you end where you've begun, you've written a circle, not an essay."
>
> Circular reasoning may or may not be a concept within the scope of your course's curriculum, but if it is, this is an excellent launchpad for such a lesson.

3. Let students know that you will be giving them a few simple questions that take only seconds to answer, but that yield short meaningful conclusions.

4. Redistribute the students' completed Body Paragraphs That Don't Stand Alone handout. Students will not be able to complete So What? handout without previously drafted body paragraphs.

5. Distribute the student handout So What?

6. Read aloud the sample thesis statement and its corresponding sample conclusions, pausing to discuss how each one gives the reader a sense of what to do or think next.

> ✒ **Peter Prickly:** If I don't summarize my points or restate my thesis, how will the reader know what they were?
>
> **Mrs. Snippy:** If you've been beginning your body paragraphs with claims and ending them by linking back to your thesis with internal conclusions, your points will be easy to detect and clearly developed. If you've failed to do so, then you're right—your reader will be lost.

7. Ask for student feedback about what they thought was the most effective sample conclusion, given the writer's thesis and body paragraphs.
8. Instruct students to transcribe their prompt and thesis in the space provided on the handout.
9. Allow approximately 20 minutes for students to complete the remainder of the handout by writing 1–2 sentence conclusions that correspond to the questions being asked above the boxes.
10. To simulate the stress of an on demand situation, you could shorten the allotted time for students to write their conclusions. Try allowing only 3 minutes per conclusion.
11. Be sure to collect students' work and set it aside for the next lesson.

Lesson extensions

- When students are finished writing their conclusions, ask them to share their personal best conclusion. It is especially helpful if all students have been writing on the same prompt because then they hear a variety of conclusions that may share their same stance on the issue.
- Challenge students—especially Peter Prickly—to find a newspaper editorial that summarizes its points or repeats its original thesis in the conclusion. You can offer buckets of extra credit, resting assured that these pieces are too short to warrant summary and these writers are too good to be circular in their reasoning.

So What?

To ensure that your conclusions do more than summarize or repeat previous information, be prepared to answer one or more of the following questions: "So what?"; "Now what?"; "If not, then what?" These questions will lead you to a brief but meaningful conclusion that doesn't risk introducing a new argument in your last paragraph but instead logically culminates your thesis.

Instructions:

1. Read aloud the sample prompt and thesis statement below and the corresponding sample conclusions.
2. Transcribe your prompt and thesis in the space provided.
3. Complete the remainder of the handout by writing 1–2 sentence conclusions that correspond with the questions being asked above the boxes.
4. When you've finished, be prepared to share your best conclusion aloud with the class.

Prompt and Thesis

Sample prompt	Your prompt
School start time should be extended until 9 a.m. for all public high schools. Plan and write an essay in which you confirm, challenge, or qualify the above assertion. Support your position with reasons and examples from your reading, studies, experiences, or observations.	

Sample thesis	Your thesis
Although starting school later means that the dismissal bell would ring later in the afternoon, the time spent in class would be more educationally valuable if classes didn't begin until 9 a.m.	

So What?

(Now that several arguments have been proven, what conclusion should the reader draw?)

Sample conclusion	Your conclusion
Starting school later in the morning could be just the boost that many students need to get more out of their high school experience. This boost is guaranteed to be stronger, longer-lasting, and more beneficial to students than the temporary kick of the triple espresso they guzzle to stay awake during first-period government.	

Now What?

(Now what should we do or think?)

Sample conclusion that answers what we should do	Your conclusion that answers what we should do
If given the chance to vote for a change in the school start time, vote in favor of helping students learn more—vote yes.	

Sample conclusion that answers what we should think	Your conclusion that answers what we should think
Sleep deprivation is a serious condition that impairs learning. If we think starting school at 9 a.m. will only indulge already lazy teenagers—we must think again.	

If Not, Then What Will Happen?

(failure to agree with my position may result in . . .)

Sample conclusion	Your conclusion
If we ignore the research that advocates a later school start time, if we ignore the students who awaken in a puddle of their own drool when the second-period bell rings, then we are ignoring the educational future of our children.	

18. Taking Time to Title: How Titles Provide Focus to an Essay

Would you have bought this book if it didn't have a title? Unlikely. It's also unlikely that you would read newspaper articles, magazine stories, or even novels if they didn't have titles. So why don't we expect student-generated essays to have titles?

Titles show ownership; they give the essay a finished quality. If written well, a title can allude to the topic of the essay while enticing the reader. If included at the top of a timed essay, a title conveys both completion and the added bit of focus needed to satisfy the evaluators.

Why do they need to do this?

Extracting a phrase or a few words from the end of an essay and slapping them at the top of an essay takes seconds. If this simple action can guarantee a sense of careful crafting for a timed essay, add focus to the piece, and possibly intrigue or entice the evaluator, these are seconds well-spent.

Why should they care?

Standardized rubrics used to assess on demand writing reward writers for being focused. When an evaluator reaches the end of an essay and hears an echo of the title, he or she receives a sense that the essay was carefully crafted—from beginning to end. Of course, the truth is that it was beautifully crafted from end to beginning.

How long will this take?

Total time: 30 minutes
> 10 minutes for a class discussion on the importance of titles
> 10 minutes to complete and discuss the first half of the student handout Taking Time to Title
> 10 minutes to complete and discuss the YOUR TURN portion of the student handout

What will you need?

Completed So What? handouts from Lesson 17
Taking Time to Title (copy for each student)

What's the procedure?

1. Begin with a discussion on the following topics as related to titles:
   - A title's role in telling us a piece of writing is well-crafted.
   - A title's role in enticing a reader to read beyond the front cover of a book or the headline.
   - A title's role in giving an "aha!" feeling at the end of an essay when suddenly the meaning of a title becomes clear.

   > 🔍 **Hint:** To demonstrate the impact of an effective title, I begin a class period with a stack of student essays in my arms. As I toss the essays, one by one onto the floor, I tell the students a good title should arouse either curiosity or interest. I explain, "If your essay were lying in the middle of the crowded hallway, would anyone stop to pick it up?" After all of the essays have been tossed, I collect them, pausing to read aloud the titles at the top of the essays. With each title, I invite the class to indicate—by shouting out "Yay!" or "Nay!"—if I should bend over to pick up the essay. It goes something like this:
   > "Literary Essay on *Julius Caesar*"
   > "NAY!"
   > "How Shakespeare Spikes the Punch Bowl"
   > "YAY!"
   > "Why Marc Antony Is the Real Villain"
   > "YAY!" "NAY!"
   > "Daggers Didn't Kill Caesar—Words Did"
   > "YAY!"
   > "English 11 Essay"
   > "NAY!"

   I conclude this demonstration by asking, "If your essay can't entice somebody to pick it up off the floor, then how can you expect the person to want to read it?"

2. Explain to students that one of the best places to extract a word or phrase for a title is the conclusion of the essay. In fact, they will be using the concluding paragraphs that they wrote previously to practice crafting titles.

> **Peter Prickly:** When we were learning about conclusions, didn't you say ending an essay where you began creates a circle, not an essay?
>
> **Mrs. Snippy:** That's true—I'm glad you were paying attention! But a title isn't a restatement of your thesis or your main points; it's an abstraction or a phrase that may not be made entirely clear until the last paragraph.

3. Distribute Taking Time to Title.

4. Read aloud the sample conclusions and their corresponding sample titles, pausing to discuss how each one arouses either the reader's curiosity or interest.

5. Remind students that when they title an essay, the title receives no punctuation—no quotation marks, no underline, no funky font changes—nothing!

6. Give students a few seconds to arrive at their own possible titles for the sample conclusions. I have deliberately avoided some of more obvious and clever titles lurking in the sample conclusions. Your class should be able to unearth at least a couple of buried titles in each conclusion.

7. Redistribute the students' completed handout So What? Students will not be able to complete the Your Turn portion of the handout without their previously written conclusions.

8. Allow 1–2 minutes tops for the students to race through the Your Turn portion of the handout, offering titles for their essay derived from their various conclusions.

9. If time allows, invite students to share their best title, followed by the conclusion that spawned it.

10. Listen for that "aha!" sensation that occurs when a concluding paragraph illuminates the intent behind an intriguing title. Emphasize this quality for the students so they can come to appreciate it and emulate it.

11. Encourage the students to respond to the *Think About It* . . . question. Point out that extracting the title from the last few lines is an efficient use of time.

Lesson extensions

- To reinforce this lesson, throughout the year I consistently award a couple of points extra credit for well-titled essay—be they timed essays or multiple-draft creations. Before I return a set of papers, I will declare on the board: "Most Titillating Titles," or "Titles That Made Me Want to Read More." What's important is to list both the names of the authors and their illustrious titles. Once this catches on—and it does—this reward can be reserved for students who might otherwise be struggling with the rigors of the writing assignments.

Seeing their name in the board and a creative phrase attached to it is some of the best encouragement one can offer.

- Ask students to rifle through their portfolios and retitle any essays that were denied the full impact of a creative title.
- Look at the sample student essays in Appendixes 7 and 8 and offer new titles—especially for the low and middle scores.

Taking Time to Title

Instructions:

1. Read aloud the sample thesis statement below, the corresponding sample conclusions, and the titles derived from them.
2. For each sample conclusion, offer another title derived from the conclusion.

REMEMBER: When you title an essay, the title receives no punctuation—no quotation marks, no underline, no funky font changes—nothing!

3. Complete the handout by creating two possible titles that could be derived from each of the conclusions you developed in So What?
4. When you've finished, be prepared to share your best titles with the class.

Sample

Thesis: Although starting school later means that the dismissal bell would ring later in the afternoon, the time spent in class would be more educationally valuable if classes didn't begin until 9 a.m.

Conclusion that answers the question "So What?"

Starting school later could be just the boost that many students need to get more out of their high school experience. This boost is guaranteed to be stronger, longer-lasting, and more beneficial to students than the temporary kick of the triple espresso they guzzle to stay awake during first-period government.

Possible titles derived from that conclusion:

1. A Beneficial Boost
2. Getting More Out of the High School Experience
3. Another title derived from this conclusion:

Conclusion that answers the question, "What should we do?"

If given the chance to vote for a change in the school start time, vote in favor of helping students learn more—vote yes.

Possible titles derived from that conclusion:

1. If Given the Chance, Vote Yes!
2. Your Vote Could Help Students Learn More
3. Another title derived from this conclusion:

_____

_____

Conclusion that answers the question, "What should we think?"

Sleep deprivation is a serious condition that impairs learning. If we think that starting school at 9 a.m. will only indulge already lazy teenagers—we must think again.

Possible titles derived from that conclusion:

1. Will We Be Indulging Lazy Teens?
2. Think Again!
3. Another title derived from this conclusion:

_____

_____

Conclusion that answers the question "What will happen if we disagree with your position?"

If we ignore the research that advocates a later school start time, if we ignore the students who awaken in a puddle of their own drool when the second-period bell rings, then we are ignoring the educational future of our children.

Possible titles derived from that conclusion:

1. Ignoring Our Children's Future
2. A Bleak Future
3. Another title derived from this conclusion:

_____

_____

Your Turn to Title Your Work

Consult the conclusions you wrote on the previous student handout So What? Remember, strive to arouse the reader's curiosity and interest with your titles.

Possible titles derived from your conclusion that answers the question "So What?"

1. _____

2. _____

Possible titles derived from your conclusion that answers the question "What should we do?"

1. _____

2. _____

Possible titles derived from your conclusion that answers the question "What should we think?"

1. _____

2. _____

Possible titles derived from your conclusion that answers the question "What will happen if we disagree with your position?"

1. _____

2. _____

Think About It . . .

Aside from the sense of "aha!" a reader gains by discovering your title in the final paragraph, why does it make logistical sense for you in a timed situation to extract a title from the last few lines you've just written?

CHAPTER 6

Coaching the Timed Essay

I used to look forward to in class writing days—plopping down in my desk chair, savoring the silence as the students scratched their pens on the paper. Then I realized that my debaters and extemporaneous speakers worked better under time constraints than my writing students because they had an internalized sense of time born out of coping with distractions.

In a debate round, debaters are given a limited amount of prep time—often in 30-second intervals. This time allotment is called out by a judge or timer in the room (e.g., "sixty seconds of prep time remaining"). One would assume that this is distracting to the debater who is thinking and scribbling notes, but, after the first few rounds, the students adapt. While debaters speak, the judge often slaps the desk or holds up fingers to announce how much time has elapsed. At first, all this commotion is terribly annoying. However, after a few rounds, the debaters develop an innate sense of what a 6-minute speech or a 3-minute rebuttal "feels" like. They'll come back from rounds and tell me that they know the timer flubbed up and was off by a minute or 30 seconds. Those seemingly distracting time signals and annoying interventions actually give them an internal pacesetter that helps them manage their speech and preparation time more efficiently and with less anxiety.

I have found that giving this gift of internal time markers to writing students is just as imperative. They feel more in control and less surprised when time begins to run out. They are able to sense when prep time is over and when the paragraphing must give way to those last 2 minutes of proofreading.

That's why I've abandoned my desk chair for an uncomfortable stool where I perch, ticking stopwatch in hand, coaching them through the intervals of a successful timed essay.

19. Actively Coaching from the Sidelines: What to Do While the Students Write

Attend any sporting event and the last thing you'll see is the coach lounging in a corner with a cup of coffee and the newspaper. As writing coaches, we need to stay in the game—attentive to what the students are doing as the clock counts down. Remaining engaged in their struggles will help us better assess what strategies they're mastering, which ones they're fumbling, and which ones need to be reviewed during the next class.

Why do they need to do this?

With only 25–40 minutes to craft an essay, students need to allot their precious time, but before they can do so, they must be able to pace themselves. Pacing oneself comes from being able to sense how much time has elapsed.

Why should they care?

Even the most creative and competent writer can be stymied by a surprise announcement of: "Two minutes remaining." Being conscious of the time allows the writer to be in control of the time. Being coached to internalize the intervals of on demand writing allows the writer to confidently stride to the next step of an essay rather than stumbling into a final paragraph that may decide one's future college.

How long will this take?

Total time: 25–45 minutes depending on which type of prompt is being practiced.

What will you need?

a writing prompt

stopwatch—preferably that sounds a beep or, if you have an LCD projector in the classroom, log onto to http://www.online-stopwatch.com/full-screen-stopwatch. Project the countdown stopwatch on the wall. It has a built-in sound feature, too.

What's the procedure?

This procedure is designed for practicing with the new SAT I 25-minute essay. You can modify it for the timed essay of your choice.

1. Announce the prompt and tell the students that they have 25 minutes to write their essay.
2. Start the stopwatch with a "beep" telling students that they should take 5 minutes to break down the prompt and roadmap their response.
3. After 5 minutes, interrupt them and announce that they have the next 15 minutes for paragraphing their essay.
4. After a total of 20 minutes have elapsed, let the beeping of the stopwatch interrupt them; then whisper that they now have 5 more minutes to finish, proofread, and create a title for the essay.
5. In the final 2 minutes, alert them with a slap on the desk to the final 2-minute warning—reminding them to proofread and insert the title.

> **Peter Prickly:** Why do you always tell us to put a title on our essays? Doesn't that seem like a waste of energy when we only have 25 minutes to write this essay?
>
> **Mrs. Snippy:** Borrowing a few words from the conclusion of your essays and inserting them at the top of the page as a title can help salvage an essay that may have wandered from the initial roadmap. A title gives focus to a piece of writing, and focus is measured on most standardized rubrics.

6. The beeping of the stopwatch is the last sound students hear before passing their papers forward.
7. Repeat this procedure 4 to 5 times, eventually letting the students monitor their intervals. At this point, my students cheer, grateful not to have me barking out commands, and I finally get to plop in the chair and collapse—grateful that the students have an internal pacesetter in place.

20. Students as Peer Coaches: A System of Student Scoring

Peer-editing and critique are nothing new; some teachers rely on them weekly, but other teachers find the practices too risky. They fear that students will only confuse and possibly mislead their peers with their feedback. However, allowing students to be responsible for evaluating each other's work contains rewards worth the risks. In 2006, a study published in *The Journal of Educational Psychology* found that "instructor concerns about peer evaluation reliability and validity should not be a barrier to implementing peer evaluations."* Sitting on the other side of the desk gives students a valuable vantage point—they learn what's being evaluated and come to emphasize those qualities in their writing.

Students often believe that the only true form of assessment comes from the teacher. But with a solid rubric and some time spent arriving at a consensus about what constitutes a particular score, or "norming" a set of papers, I learned that student writers can become effective coaches. I begin by training the coaches.

Why do they need to do this?

Sitting in the evaluator's chair gives students a different perspective on on demand writing. They begin to see that handwriting and clear organization count for more than a precisely chosen word or remembering how to use a semicolon.

Why should they care?

Two things happen after students score each other's essays. They begin to see what it takes to get a higher score, and they gain confidence in their ability to know what a high score looks like. Being able to self-assess one's work is the ultimate goal of any writing class.

How long will this take?

Total time: 60 minutes

    40 minutes for the initial "norming session"

    20 minutes—perhaps on Day 2—to score a set of papers

---

*Cho, Kwangsu, et al. "Validity and Reliability of Scaffolded Peer Assessment of Writing from Instructor and Student Perspectives." *Journal of Educational Psychology* 98, no. 4 (November 2006), 891–901.

What will you need?

Norming Session

Scoring Rubric (copy for each student)

3 sample essays (high, medium, and low scoring) from the College Board Web site www.collegeboard.com, appendix 7 or 8, or another class (copies for each student)

T-scoring template (found in Appendix 6)

scratch paper

stapler

Scoring Session

class set of ungraded student essays—preferably from another class period

scraps of paper for T-scoring

staplers

What's the procedure?

Norming Session

1. Let the students know that they will be involved in "norming" a set of papers—coming to a consensus about how to score essays using a 6-point rubric.

2. Distribute the 6-point rubric for the SAT I from the College Board (found in Appendix 2) or another assignment-specific rubric, and sample essays. The lesson works best if you deliberately select a high-, medium-, and low-performance essay for the students to score.

3. After students have had a chance to read the rubric, review it with them, asking questions like "What distinguishes a score of 4 from a 5?" or "What do you suppose 'a consistent point of view' means?" to help clarify the wording of the rubric.

4. Ask students to read and score the essays.

5. Then ask students to reveal their "official" scores as you write the results on the board and talk about why the essays received the evaluations they did. Your plot might look something like this:

Essay	Score of 1	Score of 2	Score of 3	Score of 4	Score of 5	Score of 6
RC		3	7	20	6	
PP				2	17	12
RM	1	8	22			

The chart above illustrates that 3 students gave the RC essay a 2; 7 scored it as a 3; 20 scored it as a 4, and 6 students gave the essay a 5.

6. Ideally, while the individual scores the students gave each essay may vary slightly, the class should be able to agree on which essay was a high-performing piece, which was medium, and which was low.

7. Then distribute copies of a single essay (a middle-low essay works best because it will give the students plenty of areas for improvement to comment on) and ask the students to T-score it. A T-score is a brief evaluation of a piece of writing that includes at least one compliment and one suggestion for improvement based on the rubric being used. The suggestion should reference the item on the rubric that kept the paper from achieving the next higher score on the rubric. For a T-score template and directions on how to write a T-score, see Appendix 6.

+ Score -	
compliments based on the rubric	suggestions for improvement based on the rubric

8. Emphasize that the compliments and suggestions must use the language of the rubric.

9. Collect and assess these T-scores for their accuracy to determine if the class is ready for the next session of peer evaluation.

Scoring Session

Students are now ready to score a set of student essays.

Hints:

- I usually collect and keep the timed essays my students have been writing. Of course, I've resisted the urge to grade these essays, but in a 20-minute scoring session, I can count on the students scoring a class set of papers.
- It helps if you can swap papers between class periods or ask students to write their student ID number at the top of the page rather than their names to preserve anonymity.

Prepare for a scoring session during which each essay will be read and scored at least twice.

1. Set up 3 baskets in front of the room labeled:
   a. "Read Once"
   b. "Read Twice"
   c. "Needs a Third Read"
2. Have a stack of extra scrap paper (for writing the T-scores) and staplers available next to each of the baskets in the front of the room.
3. Distribute student essays (preferably with student ID numbers rather than names) and the scraps of paper.
4. Have students read the essays and T-score on the scrap of paper.
5. Tell them that when they have finished scoring, they are to come to the front of the room and place the essays in the "Read Once" basket, after folding and stapling their T-score to the essay to hide their score.
6. Next, they take an essay from the "Read Once" basket, read it, and score the essay on the back of the attached scrap of paper.
7. They are then to peek at the previous score. If the first score matches or is within one point of the second score, the essay goes into the "Read Twice" basket, and it is finished! If there is a two-point discrepancy, the essay goes into the "Needs a Third Read" basket.
8. These steps are repeated until all of the essays have landed in either the "Read Twice" basket or the "Needs a Third Read" basket.
9. Then allow the class to debrief on what impressed them about various essays and what they discovered to be the top impediments to giving higher scores.
10. After you—or a TA—have had a chance to reconcile the scores in the "Needs a Third Read" basket, you'll want to return the essays.

> *Hint:* To return the essays, I spread them out smorgasbord style on a table and invite the students to retrieve their papers. After they've had a chance to read their T-scores, I ask them to put their name on the essays and return them to me so I can enter the scores in the grade book.

If you are planning to conduct the portfolio reflection outlined in Lesson 22, plan on saving at least 3 scored essays per student.

Lesson extensions

- After collecting the essays and recording their scores, house the essays in the classroom for the final on timed writing in Lesson 22.
- Redistribute the scored portfolio reflection essays and ask the students to peer-edit them as prescribed in Lesson 21. This exercise could generate a multiple-draft essay, allowing the students who have participated in this on demand writing unit to revisit the entire writing process.

Avoid the urge to score any essays! You will be needed as a coach: to maintain silence, answer questions about which basket to put a paper in (a question asked at least 14 times a session!), and to encourage the faster readers to take a third or fourth essay to read.

I must confess I needed 12 years of having students T-score each other's essays before I had the courage to let these scores go into the grade book as real points. I have two safety nets in place that allow me to feel comfortable with my decision:

1. Essays holistically scored on a 6-point scale receive a small number of points compared with a thoroughly drafted essay I grade that may be worth 50 or more points.
2. Students unhappy with their score are invited to meet with me before or after school within a week of having an essay returned to challenge the score. If I agree, they get the bump; otherwise, they get to revise for the score they thought they had earned.

This year I had 4 challenges (2 by the same student—probably Peter Prickly) and only 1 essay was incorrectly scored.

21. Peer-Editing: Taking a Timed Essay to a Final Draft

You may be surprised to find a lesson on peer-editing in a book on timed essay writing. On demand writing, however, doesn't have to cancel out the benefits of guiding students through the authentic writing process of drafting and revision. In fact, an on demand writing session can produce an essay that can be evaluated as a timed essay and then turned over to an editing group for consideration as a first draft.

One of the most frustrating steps of the writing process in the classroom setting is having students arrive in class without a first draft. Allowing a timed essay to serve as a rough draft ensures that all students have a complete first draft with which to participate.

Below is a peer-editing worksheet that walks students through a series of steps that begin with self-reflection and culminate with detailed scrutiny.

Why do they need to do this?

Peer-editing can be a passive activity—pass your paper on to others and count on them to find what's wrong with it and correct it. To wean students from this passivity, encourage student writers to first reflect on their essays' strengths and weaknesses and offer some direction to the peers who are about to do them the favor of editing. Meanwhile, editors should be encouraged to do more than seek and destroy problems; they should be asked to offer suggestions for improvement—thus transforming the editors into your assistant coaches.

Why should they care?

This peer-editing exercise puts a lot of responsibility on the writer to reflect and assess. Weaning students from dependency on others—peers and teachers—to tell them what to improve in a final draft is an important step to gaining competency in writing.

How long will this take?

Total time: 65 minutes

    15 minutes to arrange editing groups, return previously written essays, and explain the editing procedure

    30 minutes for verbal peer-editing

10 minutes to determine the list of specific errors that the styling editor will be searching for

10 minutes for silent scrutiny of style and mechanics

What will you need?

Editing an Essay Takes . . . Honesty, Guts, and Style (copies for each student)

first drafts of a previously written essay

copies of the scoring rubric that will be ultimately used to grade the essay (the SAT 6-point scoring rubric from Appendix 2 will work)

list of errors you want the students to watch for when editing the papers

What's the procedure?

1. Remind the students that although they've been learning strategies to help them with the demands of timed writing, they will still be expected to polish papers into final drafts. What's more, as editors, they will be exposed to each other's papers and to different degrees of success in addressing the same prompt.

2. Organize students into groups of 3—no more— and return the previously written essays to their authors.

3. Distribute Editing an Essay handout and review.

4. Allow 10 minutes of silence for each student to complete Step 1 of the handout.

5. Then ask the group to take turns reading their essays aloud and receiving feedback from group remembers. Tell them that each author has 10 minutes for this process.

> **Peter Prickly:** Why can't I just pass my paper to the people in my group?
>
> **Mrs. Snippy:** You could, but then you would be relying on others to catch all of your mistakes. Reading the essay aloud will help you hear your own slips and to self-edit.

6. Allow a total of 30 minutes for this step. This will be ample time for each student to read aloud his or her essay and to garner feedback that can be transcribed onto the editing sheet.

7. Interrupt students at 10-minute intervals to alert them to move on to the next essay. This will help keep them on task and remind them that the clock is ticking.

8. Pause to review the list of errors or stylistic concerns that you want the styling

editor to address. Ask students to record the list of errors in Step 3 of the peer-editing sheet.

9. In the last 10 minutes of class, silence should descend a second time as each essay is passed to a member of the group to be edited for style and mechanics as explained in Step 3 of the peer-editing sheet.

> **Hint:** Tailor the list of mechanical and stylistic errors to reflect those elements that you've recently taught or that are most prevalent in your students' writing.

Editing an Essay Takes . . . Honesty • Guts • Style

The HONEST writer (name):

_____

period _____

STEP 1: You have 10 minutes to complete this section
Topic (write your prompt below):

_____

_____

_____

Are you (check one)
____ **confirming**
____ **challenging**
____ **qualifying the chosen statement**
For the sake of your argument, what is your thesis?

_____

_____

_____

Briefly list the strengths and weaknesses of your essay as you see them.

+	-

What specific areas are you hoping to improve with the help of your editors?

_____

_____

Read over the scoring rubric. What score would you give your essay in its current state and why?

_____

_____

STEP 2: Read your essay aloud to your editing group members and elicit their replies to the following gutsy questions. It's up to you to write down their replies. You have 10 minutes for this.

The GUTSY editors (names):

_____

_____

- **What contributed to the overall persuasive impact of my essay?**

_____

_____

- **What detracted from the overall persuasive impact of my essay?**

_____

_____

- **What was the most memorable moment in my essay?**

_____

_____

- **Where could or should I provide more specific detail or examples?**

_____

_____

- **Where should I consider putting more commentary or analysis?**

_____

_____

- **C'mon I can take it—here are the tough questions . . .**

  Do my paragraphs logically link and develop my ideas or are they random and disconnected?

  _____

  _____

  Does my conclusion move beyond my thesis?

  _____

  _____

STEP 3: After each member of the group has shared his or her essay aloud, swap with one other styling person and complete this section. You have 10 minutes to do so.

The STYLING editor (name):

_____

This editor is responsible for the quality control of the essay.

Place [brackets] around any and B.O. in the essay.

Create a list of errors that your teacher wants you to proofread for:

_____

_____

_____

_____

_____

_____

Place an X by any of these errors as you encounter them in the essay. Remember, it's not your job to "fix" the errors—that's up to the writer!

22. Portfolio Reflections: How to Prepare On Demand Writing for the Portfolio

Just before the juniors sit for their AP exams and their first SATs in the spring and just prior to the seniors sitting for their last SAT in October, I ask the students to pause and reflect on what they know about on demand writing and to take inventory of their personal strengths and weaknesses.

This self-reflection brings a unit of on demand writing to a close, allows them to cash in on some points, and, most important, readies them for the timed challenges ahead, reassuring them that they are, in fact, prepared to meet the demands of on demand writing.

Why do they need to do this?

A unit helping students develop on demand writing skills can span a month or more. Pausing to ask the students to reflect on their experiences and to self-assess their abilities helps to drive home the lessons and have each student clear on her or his strengths and areas that need improvement.

Why should they care?

Collating all of their timed essays and seeing the trend in their scores and the overlap of comments can help students focus on the one or two areas for improvement that could significantly raise their scores.

How long will this take?

30 minutes should be ample time to return all of the papers, have students collate their essays, and complete the portfolio reflection sheet. You can assign the revised essay as homework or allow 45–50 minutes for this if it's to be done at school.

What will you need?

Students will need 3 of their previously T-scored timed essays
Portfolio Reflections (copy for each student)
Copies of a 6-point rubric (see Appendix 2) or other rubric used to score student timed-writes
Access to a computer lab (optional)

What's the procedure?

1. Return the previously scored essays.
2. Distribute Portfolio Reflections and the 6-point rubric or other rubric used to score the essays.
3. Ask students to read over the entire handout and to seek clarification before they begin responding to the questions.
4. Remind students to borrow language from the scoring rubric as they respond to the questions.
5. Students should complete questions 1 through 5 *before* they begin revising one of the essays.
6. Encourage students to select an essay that they'd enjoy revisiting in terms of topic and ideas, not necessarily an essay they received a high or low score on. Those scores have already been banked.
7. If time allows, students can begin revising their selected essay and complete the revisions for homework.

   ### 𝒫 *Hints:*
   - Rather than send the essays home for revision, I usually allow for a period in the computer lab to oversee the student revisions. It gives me a chance to assist with basic formatting issues (e.g., headings, title placement) that often arise in word-processed essays.
   - Regardless of whether the revised essay is completed at home or in class, be sure that students return to question 6 on the Portfolio Reflections before submitting their project. Their scores will and should be rather high—they now have the distinct advantage of knowing what's expected before it's being inspected *and* they've had time to plug any holes in their first hastily written draft.
   - I usually include a scoring guide at the bottom of the Portfolio Reflections that allows me to tally their previous scores and my score on their revised essay. Multiplying their revised essay score by 5 or 10 pts is my way of rewarding them for the entire project. I sometimes also hold them accountable for mechanical errors or elements of grammar or style that they have previously studied.

Sample Scoring Guide

Essay #1's combined T-Scores	_____	+	_____	=	_____
Essay #2's combined T-Scores	_____	+	_____	=	_____
Essay #3's combined T-Scores	_____	+	_____	=	_____
Revised essay score	_____	×	_____	=	_____
Total					_____

Portfolio Reflections

Instructions:

1. Collect your timed essays and read over the essays and their T-scores.
2. Select *one* essay to revise. Base your decision on the content of the essay, not the score it received. Make sure you like this topic!
3. Respond to questions 1 through 5 *before* you begin your revision. Remember to use language from the scoring rubric as you respond to the questions.
4. Revise the essay and word process the final copy.
5. Respond to the last question *after* you have revised your chosen essay.
6. Assemble this project as follows: this sheet, the revised essay, the original draft of the essay, and all other essays *attached to their T-scores*.

This project will be housed in your portfolio. Make certain that it's spiffy!

Questions Prior to Revising Your Essay (refer to the 6-point rubric!)

1. After perusing your collection of on demand writings, what are your strategies when faced with a timed essay?

_____

_____

2. What remain your personal challenges of on demand writing?

_____

_____

3. Which essay do you plan to revise and why?

_____

_____

4. What score did it receive and why?

_____

_____

5. What specifically will you do to revise the essay? Please mention *all* changes you plan to make.

After You Revise Your Essay

6. What new score would you give your essay and why? Please make references to the language of the 6-point rubric in your explanation.

CHAPTER 7

Reaching the Top of the Rubric

The previous chapters have imparted strategies designed to coach students into a passing position on a standardized rubric for on demand writing. But how can students be coached into excelling on the same rubric? The upper echelons of most standardized rubrics account for skillful syntactical variety, appropriate and varied word choice, and few, if any, mechanical errors. Essentially, the higher scores reflect sophisticated style. Style is an acquired skill set—some students enter our classrooms with sophisticated style worthy of a published writer, others arrive with the plodding style of writers experienced at filling in the blanks on worksheets.

The challenge facing us is how to coax a more sophisticated, complex style out of perfunctory writers while offering meaningful practice to the stylistically accomplished students. Making both groups aware of simple stylistic blunders like shifts in point of view is an easy first step. Improving syntactical variety through sentence modeling allows students to self-challenge based on their preexisting abilities. Encouraging students to become more verb-conscious can elevate their diction. Finally, reviewing the mechanical and stylistic errors that grammar check programs frequently miss imparts a skill that can carry over when the on demand writing gives way to multiple-draft papers.

23. Maintaining a Consistent Point of View: I OK—You Not!

Ever notice that when people are being asked their opinion on a controversial issue, they often hedge and shift from "I" statements to vague claims that contain "you"? For instance, a local politician might state: "I oppose tax cuts. You can't build infrastructure without tax revenue." Or a boss addressing a new employee dress code might claim, "I have had to revisit our dress code policy. You lose respect as professionals if you are dressed for a day at the beach." These shifts in point of view indicate a reluctance to own the statements and a resistance to be included in the claim. What's more, the replacement of "I" or "we" with "you" dilutes the impact of the statement.

Coaching students to own their arguments and to support their claims with personal examples and observations as the prompts warrant includes building an awareness of their pronoun usage.

Why do they need to do this?

When I was presenting a workshop on peer assessment of timed essays at a California Teachers of English (CATE) conference, a woman in the audience introduced herself to me as reader for the SAT I exams. She said she was glad that I had addressed the importance of avoiding the pronoun "you." She added that, as a reader, she had been instructed to take an essay down a full notch on the 6-point scale for inconsistent point of view. Ouch! That was reason enough for me both to mention this to my students and to emphasize it—repeatedly!

Why should they care?

Losing a full score on their essays because of pronoun slippage is a serious threat that's easy to avoid simply by being conscious of pronoun use (do *not* use "you") and to be sure to maintain consistency with the other pronouns.

How long will this take?

Total time: 45–50 minutes

    10 minutes to showcase sample sentences that incorrectly use "you"

    10 minutes to discuss differences between 1st and 3rd person points of view

    25–30 minutes to complete student handout and discuss answers

    30-minute homework assignment

What will you need?

I OK—You Not! (copy for each student)

What's the procedure?

1. Extract some sentences from student essays where the informal pronoun "you" has been used inappropriately. If you're at a loss, here are a few of my favorites winnowed from student papers:
   - "If you want to be prom king, you must be respected by all different types of students."
   - "If you eat dessert every day, you will not be able to fit in your chair."
   - "If you don't stop polluting, our world will be destroyed."

2. Explain how the writer overlooked who would be reading the paper—a 46-year-old female English teacher! Then ask students to write a thought bubble for the teacher reading each of the above sentences in an essay.

   Sample:
   - "If you want to be prom king, you must be respected by all different types of students."
   - Teacher's thoughts: *Wow! I didn't know that teachers could run for prom king; I'd better order that tux and polish my dance moves.*
   - "If you eat dessert every day, you will not be able to fit in your chair."
   - Teacher's thoughts: *Hey! Who told you about my 12-day ice cream binge? For your information, they do make chairs smaller than they used to.*
   - "If you don't stop polluting, our world will be destroyed."
   - Teacher's thoughts: *Who knew that I had such powers? They say that teachers change the world—I guess they are right. My excessive trips to the library are going to kill us all.*

3. Point out that the inability to know precisely who will be reading an on demand essay is a good enough reason to avoid the pronoun "you."

4. Review the prompt stems (e.g., "Citing examples from your reading, observation, and personal experience, write an essay . . . ") to the SAT I and ACT exams, underscoring the fact that the prompts *do* invite the writers to cite personal examples and observations—suggesting that the use of "I" and "we" is permissible in the context of the essay.

✒ **Peter Prickly:** I've been told by other teachers to never to use "I" in an essay.

Mrs. Snippy: No doubt, I may have been one of those teachers. If you were asked to write about WWII or Shakespeare's England it would hardly seem appropriate to use "I" since there's a good chance that you did not experience either firsthand. However, when a prompt invites you to cite personal examples or observations, it's giving you permission to use "I" or "we."

Pause to illustrate the difference between 1st person and 3rd person point of view, emphasizing two key observations:

1. 3rd person is more formal
2. 1st person and 3rd person should never be mixed

Sample:

- **The forbidden "you":** "If you want to be prom king, you must be respected by all types of students."
- **The informal 1st person:** "If I want to be prom king, I must be respected by all types of students."
- **The formal 3rd person:** "If one wants to be prom king, one must be respected by all types of students."
- **The forbidden "you":** "If you eat dessert every day, you will not be able to fit in your chair."
- **The informal 1st person:** "If I eat dessert every day, I will not be able to fit in my chair."
- **The formal 3rd person:** "If one eats dessert every day, one will not be able to fit in one's chair."
- **The forbidden "you":** "If you don't stop polluting, our world will be destroyed."
- **The informal 1st person:** "If we don't stop polluting, our world will be destroyed."
- **The formal 3rd person:** "If people don't stop polluting, the world will be destroyed."

5. Conclude your discussion with the observation that "you" is not only inappropriate given the unknown identity of the reader, but that it more than likely will

also indicate a shift in point of view from 3rd person or 1st person to 2nd person. Maintaining a "consistent point of view" is a prerequisite for the highest marks on the scoring rubrics.

> ✎ **Peter Prickly:** But what if you know who's going to be reading your paper? Sometimes you have to use "you"!
>
> **Mrs. Snippy:** On a standardized test you can't know who's going to be reading your paper. But you're right, if you know your audience, and you're giving them instructions, the pronoun "you" is permissible. Take for instance the directions on this wonderful handout I've prepared just for *you* . . .

6. Distribute I OK—You Not! Review the directions and read aloud the sample for Part I.
7. Ask students to share some of their replies. Allow 5–7 minutes for the students to respond.
8. Read aloud the directions and sample for Part II. Allow 5–7 minutes for the students to respond.
9. Call on some of the students to share their answers aloud, while the others self-correct their work.
10. Part III and Part IV can be assigned as homework or completed in class. Students should need approximately 30 minutes to rewrite the paragraph twice and to complete the mix and match section.

I OK—YOU NOT!

PART I—LET'S PLAY THE TEACHER

Instructions: Imagine that you are a teacher (scary thought, to be sure) reading a stack of essays when you come across the following sentences. Playing the role of the teacher, jot down your thoughts as you encounter the following claims. The first one is done for you.

Sample:

"If you want to get into a good college, you must perform well on standardized tests."
Teacher's thoughts: *Gee, I knew I was forgetting something! I guess I should take some tests and go to college!*

1. "You should brush up on your basic rules of punctuation before writing an essay."
    Teacher's thoughts:

    _____

    _____

2. "If you are having trouble earning passing scores on your essays, you should ask a teacher to help you assess your writing."
    Teacher's thoughts:

    _____

    _____

3. "If you read more, your writing will improve."
    Teacher's thoughts:

    _____

    _____

4. "Your bad handwriting could be the reason your essays are not passing. Slow down and remember to use capital letters at the beginning of each sentence."
    Teacher's thoughts:

    _____

    _____

Wasn't that fun? Now you can see how ridiculous it is for the reader to encounter the informal pronoun "you."

Depending on your subject, you may still want to use informal pronouns; if so, you will want to choose "I" or "we." If, however, the subject is impersonal—like WWII or photosynthesis—employ the formal pronoun "one."

PART II—VARYING THE POINT OF VIEW

Instructions: Experiment with different points of view, rewriting each of the following sentences. Underline the pronouns. The first one is done for you.

Sample:

The forbidden "you": "If you can write well on demand, you will reap benefits in college."

The informal 1st person: "If I can write well on demand, I will reap benefits in college." Or "If we can write well on demand, we will reap benefits in college."

The formal 3rd person: "If one can write well on demand, one will reap benefits in college."

1.

The forbidden "you": "You must be able to organize your thoughts quickly and roadmap a response to the essay prompt."

The informal 1st person:

_____

_____

_____

_____

The formal 3rd person:

_____

_____

_____

_____

2.

The forbidden "you": "If you prepare in advance with a brain purge, you will have plenty of examples for your essay."

The informal 1st person:

_____
_____
_____
_____

The formal 3rd person:

_____
_____
_____
_____

3.

The forbidden "you": "You should try to begin your body paragraphs with claims, not facts or observations."

The informal 1st person:

_____
_____
_____
_____

The formal 3rd person:

_____
_____
_____
_____

(Careful . . . this next one requires more than pronoun replacements.)

4.

The forbidden "you": "At the end of your essay, strive to answer the question, 'Now what?' to offer your readers food for thought."

The informal 1st person:

_____

_____

_____

_____

_____

The formal 3rd person:

_____

_____

_____

_____

_____

PART III—MAINTAINING A CONSISTENT POINT OF VIEW

Instructions: On a separate sheet of paper, rewrite the following paragraph, converting the informal pronoun "you" to the first person pronoun "I." Beware: changing pronouns may also require altering verbs.

> *You* are expected to perform on demand constantly. Employers evaluate *your* ability to respond on demand from the moment *you* first meet in the job interview. Sure, *you'll* never know the exact questions that will be put to *you* in an interview, but *you'd* be a fool not to do a little research about the company or think through a reply to the "tell us a little bit about yourself" question. While it's not uncommon for *you* to pre-think before going into a situation where *you* may have to talk on demand, it is uncommon for *you* to prepare for a situation where *you* may have to write on demand on an unknown prompt. However, preparing for an impromptu situation—oral or written—is not only possible, it's imperative.

Now rewrite the same paragraph converting the informal pronoun "I" to the formal pronoun "one."

Think About It . . .
Both the informal pronoun "I" and the formal pronoun "one" are correct as long as they are used consistently throughout an essay. Why would a writer choose to use one or the other?

PART IV—NEVER MIX AND MATCH!

Instructions: Maintaining a consistent point of view requires that you never mix and match pronouns. Correct the following sentences by rewriting them with a consistent point of view. Answers should vary!

1. Maintaining a consistent point of view in one's essay is essential for our success on the SAT.

    _____

    _____

2. If you mix and match your pronouns, the reader will be confused about one's perspective.

    _____

    _____

3. Confusing one's reader is pretty much a guarantee of a low score on your essay.

    _____

    _____

4. I have found that avoiding the pronoun "you" helps one maintain consistency and lessen confusion.

    _____

    _____

5. It doesn't matter if we use formal pronouns or informal pronouns; what matters is that one is consistent.

_____

_____

24. Improving Syntactical Variety: Sentence Modeling

Not many fashion models were born flawless. With a few enhancements and a bit of airbrushing, however, models become images to envy.

Not many students were born with spectacular syntax. Not all are willing to spend the hours at the mental gym, reading highbrow authors and generating sophisticated syntactical patterns. All, however, are capable of diagnosing their flaws and emulating the great writers who strut their sentence structure and make it look effortless.

Why do they need to do this?
Complex sentence structure indicates complex thought patterns. Varied sentence structure demonstrates conscious choice in style. Superior writers are in command of their style rather than coming by it accidentally. These exercises in sentence modeling encourage students to first become aware of sentence structure in the prose they read, then in the prose they write, and finally to emulate professional writers as a means of manipulating sentence structure.

Why should they care?
Achieving upper scores on any of the standardized tests requires being able to "demonstrate syntactical variety." If students are having trouble catapulting their scores past passing into the superior range, they should consider taking modeling seriously.

How long will this take?
20–30 minutes for students to complete the worksheet. If you decide to call on students to share their imitations, allow for additional time.

Allow 2 days to collect sentences gathered by the students and to compile a modeling worksheet (optional)

You can also hold daily sentence modeling sessions of 5–7 minutes. The session can be used as a convenient "sponge" activity to quiet the class as you take roll. It can also serve as a review of certain rules of punctuation and grammar.

What will you need?

collection of syntactically splendid sentences that you've gathered from your favorite readings or the literature currently assigned to the students

Modeling Morrison, Simulating Shelley, or Rhetorical Reflections (copies for each student) (optional)

What's the procedure?

Day One

1. Write one of your syntactically splendid sentences on the board. Imitate the sentence and challenge the students to do the same.

Sample:

- The woman emerged, slowly and deliberately, from the black smudge of a car.
  —Don DeLillo, *Cosmopolis*
  The dog emerged, wet and shivering, from the greasy smudge of a pond.

- His hair was dead and thin, almost feathery on top of his head.
  —Harper Lee, *To Kill A Mockingbird*
  His fur was damp and matted, almost clumped on top of his head.

- Holding firmly to the trunk, I took a step toward him and then my knees bent, and I jounced the limb.
  —John Knolls, *A Separate Peace*
  Biting tightly on the rope, the dog took a step back and then his jaw strained, and he broke the tether.

Don't be afraid to consult your favorite beach-book author:

- Mercifully, Brunette's path took him outside the courtyard of the hospital where he had brief glimpses of sky and blossoming trees; he wished he could somehow store up the beauty of the plump clouds and take it with him.
  —Donna Leon, *Friends in High Places*
  Circuitously, the dog's path led him inside the alley of the restaurant where he smelled the odors of hamburger and rotting chicken; he wished he could somehow store up the joy of his saturated senses and take it with him.

2. It may help if you underline the key elements (e.g., a verb clause, a prepositional phrase, etc.) that students need to imitate. It may also help to give them a subject (e.g., spirit week, prom, college applications, etc.) to use in their imitation.

3. To get students noticing syntax and appreciating complex sentences, assign homework that asks them to extract sentences from their readings that are "syntactically splendid" or snazzy. The only criterion is no simple subject-verb sentences.

> 🔎 **Hint:** Resist the urge to ask students to model the sentences they extracted for homework lest they migrate toward short, simple sentences. Instead, tell them that the most syntactically splendid sentences will be selected for the class to model—then they will vie with one another for the bragging rights to find the most complex sentences. Meanwhile, this simple homework exercise of hunting for complex sentences has students reading with an eye and an ear to syntactical structure.

Day Two

Compile a worksheet using the sentences the students extracted. Invite students to emulate the author's syntax on the worksheet you've compiled. If students are reading Toni Morrison's *Beloved*, Mary Shelley's *Frankenstein*, or Andrea Lunsford's *Everything's an Argument*, they can use the worksheets below.

> 🔎 **Hint:** When students submit essays or exams written about one of the novels they've been modeling, I assign a portion of their essay grade to sentence modeling and ask them to underline 2–5 modeled sentences in their essays. For example, an essay on the theme of nature vs. nurture in *Frankenstein* will also contain 3 underlined sentences modeled after Mary Shelley's syntax.

Modeling Morrison

STEP 1: Select a topic (e.g., the weather, baseball, prom, etc.):

STEP 2: Demonstrate your modeling skills and imitate the structure of the following sentences. The first sentence has a sample imitation written for you.

Example: They heard the voice first—later the name.
They saw the clouds first—later the lightening.

Your version:

1. Too tired to move, she stayed there, the sun in her eyes making her dizzy.

    _____

    _____

    _____

2. She smiled then and Denver's heart stopped bouncing and sat down—relieved and ease full like a traveler who had made it home.

    _____

    _____

    _____

3. The stone had eaten the sun's rays but was nowhere near as hot as she was.

    _____

    _____

    _____

4. She looks at him: the peachstone skin, the crease between his ready, waiting eyes and sees it—the thing in him, the blessedness, that has made him the kind of man that can walk in a house and make the women cry.

    _____

    _____

    _____

5. The same adoration from her daughter (had it been forthcoming) would have annoyed her; made her chill at the thought of having raised a ridiculously dependent child.

_____

_____

_____

Extra Credit for super models only . . .

Even if the whole farm—every tree and grass blade of it dies. The picture is still there and what's more, if you go there—you who never was there—if you go there and stand in the place where it was, it will happen again; it will be there for you, waiting for you.

Simulating Shelley

STEP 1: Select a topic (e.g., the weekend, the Super Bowl, work, etc.):

_____

STEP 2: Demonstrate your modeling skills and imitate the structure of the following sentences. The first sentence has a sample imitation written for you.

Example: To examine the causes of life, we must first understand death.
To enjoy the relaxation of the weekend, we must first indulge in food.

Your version:

1. Mingled with this terror, I felt the bitterness of disappointment.

_____

_____

2. I was like the Arabian who had been buried with the dead and found a passage to life, aided only by one glimmering and seemingly ineffectual light.

_____

_____

3. The moon gazed on my midnight labours, while, with unrelaxed and breathless eagerness, I pursued nature to her hiding places.

_____

_____

4. Who shall conceive the horrors of my secret toil as I dabbled among the unhallowed damp graves or tortured the living animal to animate the lifeless clay.

_____

_____

Extra Credit for super models only . . .

It was a bold question, and one which has ever been considered as a mystery, yet with how many things are we on the brink of becoming acquainted, if cowardice or carelessness did not restrain our inquiries.

Student Handout

Rhetorical Reflections

STEP 1: Select a topic (e.g., eating, shopping, studying, etc.):

_____

STEP 2: Demonstrate your modeling skills and imitate the structure of the following sentences. The first sentence has a sample imitation written for you.

Example: Life is too short to belabor the obvious.
Studying is too important to forfeit the opportunity.

Your version:

1. Moving from stated reason to claim, we see that the warrant is a silly and selfish principle.

_____
_____
_____

2. Lack of logic produces a chaotic, arbitrary world, like that of the Queen of Hearts in *Alice in Wonderland*.

_____
_____
_____

3. Arguments can't be stamped out like sheet metal panels; they have to be treated like living things—cultivated, encouraged, and refined.

_____
_____
_____

4. Arguments serve too many purposes, too many occasions, and too many audiences to wear one suit of clothes.

_____
_____

EXTRA CREDIT for super models only . . .

When it comes to making claims, many writers stumble—facing issues squarely takes thought and guts.

25. Self-Diagnosis of Sloppy Syntax: Reworking Original Sentences

These exercises invite students to become conscious of their own syntax and aware that they have choices in how they lay down their words. These diagnostic exercises can be used to reinforce elements of grammar already being taught (e.g., the prepositional phrase, adverbs, etc.).

Why do they need to do this?

Being able to self-diagnose one's own lackluster sentence patterns is the ultimate goal of any exercise in style. Asking students to self-reflect on the work they've already generated in their writing portfolios invites them to individualize their instruction. Some will be up for the sophisticated challenge of improving the complexity of their sentence structure, while others will simply be converting "to be" verbs to more vivid choices. Either way, they are making improvements.

Why should they care?

These exercises can be applied independent of a teacher or tutor. These diagnostic tools can be packed off to college, where autonomy is not only encouraged, it's demanded.

How long will this take?

Total time: 50–55 minutes

If using the prescribed diagnoses listed in the exercise, approximately 40 minutes will be needed for all students to extract and rework 10 sentences.

Allow an additional 10 or 15 minutes for sharing some of the more splendid revisions aloud.

What will you need?

Students will need a recently written essay or an old piece of writing from their portfolio

Self-Diagnosis of Sloppy Syntax (copy for teacher only)

What's the procedure?

1. Have students pull out an old piece of writing from their portfolio. Preferably something they've written in class, like a timed essay or an exam.

2. Have them block out 10 sentences to examine. Ask them to number the sentences.
3. On a clean, lined sheet of paper ask them to number every 4th line 1 through 10. This will serve as their revision paper where they can rewrite each of the 10 sentences they blocked out in their original document.
4. Establish a method, like the one in the self-diagnosis handout or portions of it, for them to recognize and revise their less-than-spectacular sentences.

> $\mathcal{P}$ **Hint:** I prefer to read the diagnostic directions from the handout rather than distribute them to students. This allows me to set the pace and pick and choose the diagnostic areas I want to concentrate on.

5. Refer students to their revised list of sentences. Ask them to reassemble their 10 sentences into a cohesive unit.
6. Call on individual students and ask them to share their most spectacular new sentence by reading aloud the "before" and "after" versions of the sentence.
7. Before collecting the final draft, ask students to place an asterisk next to 2 sentences that proudly display syntactical improvements.

Lesson extensions

- During an in class writing assignment—say a practice timed-write—ask students to emulate a chosen sentence at least once in their essay.
- Of course, this is a great time to introduce the ills of dangling and misplaced modifiers.
  These mistakes can be fun to make and then correct:
  - Misplaced Modifier
    Crumpled and coffee-stained, the student turned in her essay.
  - Dangling Modifier
    Shouting with joy, the last essay was written.

Self-Diagnosis of Sloppy Syntax

Remind your students that they are to revise their sentences on a clean sheet of lined paper, and that each sentence they improve should correspond numerically to the 10 sentences they've chosen to revise.

Diagnose:	Circle the 1st word of any sentence that begins with the same word as another.
Improve:	Choose one of the sentences to re-order and rewrite it next to the corresponding number on the clean sheet of paper.
Diagnose:	Draw a square around the verbs in each sentence.
Improve:	Experiment with moving one verb before its subject. This may require changing the verb's ending. Transcribe the revised sentence on the clean sheet next to its corresponding number.
Diagnose:	A weak, lackluster verb.
Improve:	Replace it with a vivid verb and transcribe the sentence onto the list.
Diagnose:	Find a sentence that ends with a prepositional phrase.
Improve:	Move the phrase to the beginning or middle of the sentence and transcribe the sentence on the appropriate line on your paper.
Diagnose:	Search for 2 remaining sentences that can be combined.
Improve:	Using a semicolon or a comma and a coordinating conjunction, combine them into a compound or complex sentence, and transcribe the new sentence onto the list.

26. Vivifying Verbs: Improving Diction by Carefully Selecting Verbs

In preparing my students for their AP Language and Composition exam, I have struggled with ways to improve their working vocabulary on the eve of the test. The College Board's prescribed curriculum doesn't allow for extensive vocabulary building. Oftentimes, the students have jammed and crammed high-powered SAT vocabulary into their brains for their exams—but knowing definitions and being able to use words effectively are distinctly different.

I, therefore, have settled on improving my students' vocabulary by having them focus on carefully selecting verbs with which they're already familiar.

Why do they need to do this?

Verbs, unlike strings of adjectives, are much more efficient in conveying vivid images and offering illustration. In on demand writing situations, the stopwatch does not allow for long reflection about precisely the right word or scrolling through a thesaurus. Verbs are simple, familiar words that, if chosen carefully, can up the ante on any student's bet of scoring higher on a standardized rubric.

On the SAT I and the ACT exams, students are invited to cite examples from their reading. Most students will do so by stating that a particular author "uses" a theme or idea. This portion of analysis often lacks the vivid writing of the personal anecdotes that populate the rest of the essay. A few carefully selected verbs can make the inclusion of a literary or nonfiction example as compelling as a personal story.

Why should they care?

The highest scores on standardized rubrics for both the SAT I and the ACT essay tests demand that word choice be "varied and precise." Unless students are prepared to expand beyond basic utilitarian verbs like "uses" or "contains," then their scores will remain stagnant—below the superior distinction.

Studying a relatively small list of already familiar verbs is also considerably easier than memorizing a list of a thousand SAT vocabulary words and practicing their accurate and effective use.

How long will this take?

Total time: 30–60 minutes

30 minutes for brainstorming the list of verbs with the class (to eliminate this

step, use the compiled list of verbs on the teacher resource sheet)

10 minutes for students to craft their sentences

20 minutes for students share their variations aloud

What will you need?

Vivid Verbs (optional)

What's the procedure?

1. Ask students to brainstorm for vivid substitutes for the verb "uses" in the following sentence:

> The author *uses* color in her novel to show the characters' moods.

Write the sentence on the board and create a list of alternative verbs.

> $\mathcal{P}$ **Hint:** I have found that asking the students to brainstorm the list of alternative verbs on the whiteboard in class is preferable to asking them to do so at home where most will simply consult their computer's thesaurus and return with identical lists of the same tired 3 or 4 words.

2. Whip around the room, asking each student to repeat the sentence above, replacing the verb "uses" with one of the words brainstormed. Caution them that this may require changing the word order of the sentence or altering other elements of the sentence (e.g., The author *steeps* her novel in color . . .).

3. After exhausting the initial word list, extend the challenge by either adding a second sentence to the first or by giving students a sentence that contains two opportunities to dip into the word list. For example:

> The writer *creates* a scene by *using* dialogue.

4. Encourage students to select verbs that are metaphorically compatible for use in the same sentence.
> *Samples:*
>> The writer quilts a scene by stitching in bits of dialogue.
>> The writer cultivates a scene by planting lines of dialogue.
>> The writer concocts a scene by folding in dialogue.

5. Depending on the literature and terminology being studied in class, you can offer students a variety of sentences for them to complete with vivid verbs. For instance, when studying tonal analysis, I gave my students the following incomplete sentence:

The author ＿＿＿＿＿＿＿＿＿＿＿＿＿＿ a ＿＿＿＿＿＿＿＿＿＿＿＿＿＿ tone
                        vivid verb for creates   ***tonal adjective***

by ＿＿＿＿＿＿＿＿＿＿＿＿＿＿ ing diction like " ＿＿＿＿＿ " and " ＿＿＿＿＿ ."
           vivid verb for use

Sample responses:

The author *summons* a *fearful* tone by *calling upon* diction like "eerie" and "trembling."

The author *furnishes* a *fearful* tone by *ornamenting* her description with diction like "eerie" and "trembling."

Lesson extension

As said many times over in this section, raising student consciousness of stylistic choices is the primary purpose of these exercises. With that in mind, it is beneficial to occasionally instruct students to underline the verbs in one of their compositions or even in a short homework assignment—then invite them to replace a lackluster verb or two.

Vivid Verbs

Below is a list of verbs that might replace "use" or "make":

▸ ornament, decorate, adorn, furnish

▸ whip up, concoct, fold in, blend

▸ scatter, sow, cultivate

▸ formulate, inoculate, inject

▸ reinforce, wield, bolster, fortify

▸ sprinkle, shower, sling, splatter, dab

▸ call upon, summon, announce

▸ weave, quilt, stitch, braid

▸ populate, impregnate

▸ employ, work

▸ steep, brew, infuse

27. Seven Deadly Sins of Style: Catching Errors That Impede a Reader's Understanding

Whether it's a scoring rubric for an AP English exam or a junior college placement test, the advice given to holistic readers is to consistently reward writers for what they do well and to dock their score for mechanical errors only if those errors accumulate and impede the reader's understanding.

What follows is a list of 7 mechanical errors that are guaranteed to impede a reader's understanding. Since grammar check is not available to students when they are in an on demand writing situation, students do need to learn to avoid these errors. What makes these errors even more troublesome is that grammar check will not alert a writer to these mistakes because grammar check cannot intuit the intent of the writer—even in a multiple-draft essay.

Thus, students could be making these errors even in a final draft and not know it. Coaching them to anticipate these errors has a payoff for both their on demand writing experiences as well as their word processed writing.

Why do they need to do this?
Errors that impede a reader's understanding of an essay—that is to say, mistakes that make a reader stop and start throughout the text, are punishable by lowering the essay 1–2 ranks.

Why should they care?
An occasional misspelled word is a forgivable sin; failing to underline the title of the novel *Frankenstein* could mean that an entire paragraph or essay is misconstrued as being about a character, not a book. The 7 errors listed below demand student attention because they distract the reader's attention.

How long will this take?
Total time: 65 minutes
> 45–50 minutes to explain and illustrate the 7 deadly sins
> 10–15 minutes for peer assessment of essays using the 7 deadly sin checklist

What will you need?
Seven Deadly Sins Example Set
The Seven Deadly Sins of Style Checklist (copy for each student)

What's the procedure?

1. Extract sample sentences from student work that illustrate each of the 7 errors or use the teacher resource Example Set.

2. Ask students to take notes, copying down the sample sentences and correcting the errors as you explain the governing rule of style or mechanics behind each error.

3. Distribute The Seven Deadly Sins of Style Checklist. The list includes symbols that students can use to indicate a particular error.

4. Ask students to review a piece of writing—either their own or a partner's—scouring for the 7 deadly sins.

5. Designate how many points you want each sin to be worth (e.g., of a total possible 30 points, each run-on sentence may cost the writer 2 points).

> ○ **Hint:** After an essay has been graded, I often distribute the essay for revision and regrade the essay on the basis of the 7 deadly sins. Thus, students are rewarded for the content and structure of their essay before we both take turns combing through the text for mechanical and stylistic blunders.

Seven Deadly Sins Example Set

1. **Commas with coordinating conjunctions.**
   Hamlet sulks around the castle, and he ignores his family and friends.
   Comma needed

   Hamlet sulks around the castle and ignores his family and friends.
   No comma needed

Grammar check won't catch this common run-on because the computer can't anticipate the function of the conjunction in the sentence. I ask students to read their essays backward, isolating the words "and," "but" and "so." Then I ask them to determine whether what lies on either side of the conjunction is an independent clause—if so, they are told to place a comma before the conjunction. If not—leave it alone.

2. **Proper punctuation of titles.**
   Hamlet is bold and provocative.
   Underlining Hamlet indicates the subject is the play, not the man.

   I did not sing Like a Virgin!
   Placing quotations around "Like a Virgin" clarifies that the writer is referencing a song, not a manner of singing.

Grammar check has no way of knowing if a writer is referring to the title of the work or the character; the reader will be equally confused if one says: "Frankenstein is elegant" or "Beowulf is boring."

> ✏ **Peter Prickly:** How come we have to underline the titles of books and plays? I see the titles italicized on your handouts and in our exercises?
> **Mrs. Snippy:** Underlining words was the symbol for telling the typesetter to italicize words. In today's era of word processing, you have the option of italicizing or underlining titles—as long as you are consistent.

For on demand writing situations you must underline titles—try as you might, you cannot italicize with a pen.

3. **Apostrophes: possession vs. contraction**

It's hard drive broke!

Translation: It is hard drive broke! This does not make sense!

Its hard drive broke!

Translation: The hard drive is broken! This is sad!

Both "it's" and "its" are viable, correct choices given their placement. Clarification is easier if you first explain to your students that they are accustomed to using apostrophes in contractions and to show possession with nouns. Then explain how possessive pronouns, like "his" or "her" never use apostrophes. Therefore, when using "its" to show possession, never use an apostrophe. Reserve the apostrophe usage with it's for the contraction form of "it is."

4. **Verb tense: consistency**

Hamlet sulked around his castle, then he kills a few people.

The verb-tense inconsistency confuses the reader. It is particularly bothersome when writing about literature—which most on demand prompts invite writers to do. Literature, like film and other art forms, needs to be written about in the present tense.

> ✒ **Peter Prickly:** Why do we have to write about books in the present tense? I should be able to say that Hamlet killed his uncle because I finished the play, and the uncle is definitely dead.
>
> **Mrs. Snippy:** We use the present tense to write about literature because for someone somewhere the action is happening for the very first time. "Hamlet is a perplexed young man" is still correct even though by now you know that Hamlet is dead as a ducat.

Once again, writers cannot rely on grammar check to catch this error in tense, since the computer cannot distinguish between examples gathered from literature and those borrowed from experience.

5. **Pronoun/antecedent agreement**

Everyone should improve their proofreading skills.
The subject of this sentence and its pronoun are in disagreement. "Everyone" is singular; the pronoun "their" is plural.

Someone is a stickler for their grammar rules.
The subject of this sentence and its pronoun are in disagreement. "Someone" is singular; the pronoun "their" is plural.

Native English speakers cannot trust their ears when struggling to make their vague subjects (everyone, anyone, someone, everybody, etc.) agree with their pronouns. Attributable in large part to our loss of this rule in speech, student writers will struggle to find agreement. There are, however, two ways of coaching students to cure this agreement problem.

First, if they use specific subject, the problem is unlikely to occur. I point out that journalists are instructed to avoid vague subjects in their writing because it leads to the awkward "his or her" construction, which also uses more ink.

Students should improve their proofreading skills.
The subject of this sentence and its pronoun are in agreement. "Students" is plural; the pronoun "their" is plural.

Mrs. Prickly is a stickler for her grammar rules.
The subject of this sentence and its pronoun are in agreement. "Mrs. Prickly" is singular and female; the pronoun "her" is singular and female.

Second, if the subject cannot be replaced, then substitute an androgynous name like "Pat" or "Chris" for the anyone, someone, everybody, etc. Then the ear should catch the error and allow the writer to make the proper choice.

Everyone should improve their proofreading skills
Substitute "Chris" for "everyone" and trust your ear to make the pronouns agree:
Chris should improve his or her proofreading skills.

Somebody is a stickler for their grammar rules.
Substitute "Pat" for "somebody" and trust your ear to make the pronouns agree: Pat
is a stickler for his or her grammar rules.

Finally, I coach my students to keep their subject plural when possible to avoid the
cumbersome "his or her" construction.

6. Commas after dependent clauses

Forgetting to signal the attachment of dependent clause to its independent clause
will cause the reader to misread the sentence the first time through, forcing the
reader to reread it. This impedes the reader!

As I read *Hamlet* I fell asleep.
This sentence must be reread to capture its intent.

As I read *Hamlet*, I fell asleep.
The dependent clause is attached to the independent clause with a comma.

Students will benefit from the following distinction: When a dependent clause appears before an independent clause, attach it to the main clause with a comma. Keep
your commas at home when a dependent clause follows an independent clause.

As I read *Hamlet*, I fell asleep.
This sentence is correctly punctuated.

I fell asleep as I read *Hamlet*.
This sentence is correctly punctuated, too!

7. Awkward "is because" construction

Usually indicative of the passive voice as well as an awkwardly constructed sentence, the phrase "is because" is an easy one to coach students to eradicate from their essays, especially after they've been introduced to the stench of B.O. in Chapter 2.

The reason I like Hamlet is because he is witty.
awkward!

I like Hamlet because he is witty.
better!

The reason that many writers make these errors is because grammar check won't correct them.
awkward!

Many writers make these errors because grammar check won't correct them.
better!

The Seven Deadly Sins of Style Checklist

Instructions: Read the essay and place a √ by those items detected in the text. As you encounter a particular error, indicate where in the essay the error occurs by marking it with the proper proofreading symbol.

√	"Sin" Annotation	Explanation
	R.O.	Commas with coordinating conjunctions
	novels/plays	Proper font (italic) of book title and play
	"poems/essays"	Proper punctuation (quotation marks) around poem and essay titles
	↓s	Possession vs. contractions (its vs. it's)
	tense	Verb tense (consistency/present tense—literature)
	AGR	Pronoun/antecedent agreement
	↑	Commas after dependent clauses
	AWK	Awkward "is because" construction

CHAPTER 8

Practice That Can Make You Nearly Perfect

A one-day exercise in thesis construction or a 30-minute lesson in syntax is unlikely to polish your students' writing abilities to perfection. Practice—and lots of it—is almost certainly a more effective means of ensuring that students keep their prose buffed to a high luster.

The exercises in this chapter are not unique to timed-writing situations. They can be used to improve writing whether or not a stopwatch is involved. The aim of these lessons is not to teach students new strategies but to reinforce concepts that can strengthen all of their writing. Students can never get enough practice in being specific, infusing facts creatively, countering arguments logically, and reading analytically.

28. Strive to Specify: Converting Vague Phrases into Vivid Examples

Arguably, the flaw most easily remedied in student writing is also the one most students will stubbornly resist correcting—being vague.

Students often think they are being specific when they mention an example. If they state, for instance, "Math is difficult for many students," they may assume they're being specific. But once they're shown the sentence "Trig was so hard that my bother Matt nearly dropped out of school," they begin to see the difference.

Inviting students to revisit some of their writing and to infuse more specifics is a simple yet important exercise in their becoming more autonomous self-editors.

Why do they need to do this?

Being more specific not only helps students make their writing more interesting and memorable, it also helps them avoid basic lapses in logic like begging the question and circular reasoning. When a specific example is offered rather than a vague reference, it's more likely that commentary or explanation will precede or follow. Thus, encouraging detailed examples results in well-developed essays.

Why should they care?

When an evaluator holistically reads a student's essay at a brisk pace, specific, vivid examples stand a greater chance of being remembered and credited to the student's score.

How long will this take?

Total time: 40–50 minutes

    10 minutes to work with the sample sentence on the board and to discuss the importance of specific detail

    15–20 minutes for students to complete the student handout

    5 minutes for partners to swap sentences

    Optional 10–15 minutes for students to share aloud some of their improved sentences

What will you need?

Strive to Specify (copy for each student) and/or a list of vague, lackluster sentences extracted from a recent batch of student writing

What's the procedure?

> 🔎 *Hint:* I often begin this lesson by asking students to recall a recent essay or story read in class. I then encourage them (usually for participation points) to recall specific details from the piece of writing (e.g., What kind of shoes was the robber wearing? What kind of backpack did the student have?, etc.).
>
> I then ask why they remembered these bits of information given that they didn't have to—no tests or quizzes were planned. Answers will vary, but, in essence, students reveal that they couldn't help but remember because the details painted a picture in their minds.
>
> Next, I ask why painting a picture in the reader's mind would be a valuable goal in an on demand writing exercise—why would they want their reader to exit their essay with lingering images from their examples?
>
> The answer is simple. If their examples are remembered, the writer receives credit on the scoring rubric.
>
> Once we've established *why* they should care about being more specific, I proceed with this lesson and frequent nagging reminders to strive to specify!

1. Tell the class that today you are going to reveal the single most important component of writing well: being specific.
2. Begin the class by writing a sample lackluster sentence on the board—either one from the subsequent student handout or preferably one from a recent batch of student writing.
3. Underline the portions of the sentence that could benefit from being made more specific.
4. Challenge students to offer specifics for the underlined portions of the sentence.
5. Challenge them a second time to be even more specific than the first attempt (see the sample sentence on the student handout for an example).
6. Distribute Strive to Specify and review the directions and the sample sentences.
7. Allow 15–20 minutes for students to complete the worksheet.
8. Tell students to swap papers with a partner and complete the Can You Top That? portion of the handout.
9. After 5 minutes, ask students to return the papers to their original owners.

10. Ask for volunteers who claim their partners "topped that!" to read aloud their specified version of the lackluster sentence followed by their partner's more specific rendition. Give credit to both students—one for recognizing vivid, concrete detail and the other for creating it.

Lesson extensions

- As a follow-up, I will frequently begin a class session with a vague, lackluster sentence extracted from a recent batch of student writing and encourage students to strive to make the sentence more specific. Then I announce a Pop Quiz! on being more specific and distribute 3 lackluster sentences that need help. I usually give students 10 minutes tops to improve the sentence and then collect their work. If time allows, I'll read aloud a few of the improved versions and ask the class if they think there's still room for improvement.

- To encourage self-editing, I will return an ungraded piece of writing to my students and tell them that a portion of their grade will be based on their ability to make 3 of their sentences more vivid and specific. They are to underline the 3 sentences they deem vague. The improved sentences tend to be longer and are unlikely to fit scrawled above the old, so I ask them to rewrite each of the sentences on a separate sheet of paper and attach that to their original work.

Strive to Specify

Instructions:

1. Read the sample lackluster sentence and its improved versions. Note that the example is now more vivid—painting a picture in your mind's eye!
2. Infuse specific details into each of the lackluster sentences in the exercise below.
3. Once you're finished, pass your paper to a partner and see if he or she can top your first attempt at being specific.

Sample
The vague phrases/words that need to be specified have been italicized.

Lackluster sentence:
Most *students* would rather be *doing something else* besides *going to class*.

An improved version:
Most seniors would rather be at the beach than in English class.

An even better version—now with VIVID specifics!
Most seniors would rather be tossing a Frisbee at the beach than struggling with semicolons in English class.

Your Turn
Infuse specific details into each of the following lackluster sentences. The vague phrases/words that need to be specified have been italicized for you.

1. Sometimes *my mind wanders* while I'm writing *an essay.*

2. *I am often surprised* when I receive *a bad grade* on *an essay.*

_____

_____

3. Many *students* would rather *argue about their grade* than *work hard.*

_____

_____

4. Many *teachers* seem *to grade papers arbitrarily.*

_____

_____

5. *Grading practices* can vary from *class to class.*

_____

_____

6. Many *teachers* award *extra credit* to compensate *underachieving students.*

_____

_____

7. Some *students work hard* yet still fail to get *a good grade.*

_____

_____

8. Sometimes *students* neglect to check *what the teacher is grading them on.*

_____

_____

9. Often *participation* in *a class is worth more* than a student will think.

_____

_____

10. Being clear on the *teacher's expectations* can ensure *success in a class.*

_____

_____

Can You Top That?

Pass your paper to a partner and challenge her or him to improve on the sentences above.

Think About It . . .

Granted, being more specific makes your writing more vivid in the reader's mind. Why is this especially valuable in a timed essay that will be read holistically at a brisk pace?

29. Actual Factual Impromptu: Infusing Facts and Stats in Interesting Ways

My impromptu and extemporaneous speakers on the debate team are not only expected to include specific data in their speeches, they also are expected to do so in artful, memorable ways. Seeing them transfer these techniques to their persuasive writing has prompted me to coach my writing students on how to include data in their writing in ways that will get the facts noticed as well as aid in developing their thesis.

Some on demand writing situations—like AP exams and the International Baccalaureate—give the test-taker a fact-laden piece of material to read and synthesize, with the writer being expected to infuse facts or statistics into the response. Students well versed in a particular subject area may also wish to use some of their specific knowledge in response to a general prompt. For instance, a student with a passion for biology may wish to use some of her specific knowledge of the animal kingdom when responding to an aphorism by Stephen Jay Gould that questions the morality of nature.

When a writer does include specific knowledge, he or she wants those facts to have impact. Whether it's a test-taking situation or a persuasive essay, an overabundance of facts and statistics can cancel out their significance; similarly, if the facts are simply stated, they risk losing their impact by essay's end.

Why do they need to do this?
Including facts and statistics is often necessary in academic writing. Being able to artfully include the facts makes them more memorable and adds impact.

Why should they care?
Essays that are holistically scored need to ensure that the information being presented is recalled by the reader as she or he is about to determine a score. Creatively infusing facts and figures into a piece of writing can give those bits of information the necessary staying power to be remembered at the end of the reading.

How long will this take?
Total time: approx 60 minutes, depending on class size

10 minutes to read over the directions and the sample strategies

5 minutes per student to deliver an impromptu presentation (note: students not coached in public speaking will only use 1.5–2 minutes)

What will you need?

Actual Factual Impromptu Speech (copy for each student)

Actual Factual Impromptu Speech Sample Topics (or topics of your choice), cut and placed in an envelope

Actual Factual Impromptu Speech Scoring Rubric

3 x 5 cards or small scraps of paper for students to scribble notes

What's the procedure?

1. Begin by illustrating that a fact or statistic that is stated creatively has a better chance of being remembered than one that is just stated.

    > 🔎 **Hint:** I like to begin with a string of rhetorical questions and a fact. For instance, I might ask: "What percent of communication do you think is nonverbal? 5 percent? Wrong. 25 percent? Wrong again. 75 percent? Wrong still. 95 percent of communication is nonverbal." Then I would ask why that phrasing had greater impact than if I had simply stated that 95 percent of communication is nonverbal.

2. Explain that the class will learn how to introduce facts effectively by giving short impromptu speeches in which they are asked to incorporate a fact creatively. Distribute Actual Factual Impromptu Speech and review the sample illustrations on how to infuse facts creatively into a speech or an essay.

3. Ask students to read the directions under Your Turn and then turn over the handout. Distribute index cards or scraps of paper for the students to make notes on during their preparation time.

4. Pass around the envelope with the topics and remind the class that each one is to pull 3 strips but can choose the one topic on which she or he wants to speak.

5. Give each student at least 2 minutes to prepare his or her speech after drawing a topic.

6. You can ask for a volunteer (or bribe a student with extra credit) to demonstrate a sample impromptu speech.

    > 🔎 **Hint:** I usually have a student "on deck"—preparing his speech in the hallway—while another student is speaking. This may mean that the student on deck gets slightly more than 2 minutes to prepare, but it avoids the awkward lag-time between speeches. If a speaker is woefully

under the 2-minute mark, then I kill some time with an oral critique of what the speaker did well to ensure that the "on deck" student has at least the promised 2 minutes to think.

7. Encourage students to plug into one of the signposting strategies taught in Chapter 2 as they prepare their speeches.
8. Give each student 5 minutes to speak. Do not assess a penalty if less time is used.
9. Remind students that only those who incorporate the fact into their speech in a creative, memorable way will be eligible for the "+" or the best grade.
10. Using the √ +/− system, evaluate as many speakers as you can in the class period.

   🔍 **Hint:** If your students are unaccustomed to being asked to perform public speaking exercises in your class, you can offer encouragement by simply awarding credit/no credit for participating in the exercise. Those students who succeed in incorporating their *fact* into their speech in a creative, memorable way could then be eligible for extra credit.

Actual Factual Impromptu Speech

In this lesson, you will be in infusing a fact into a 5-minute impromptu speech (sounds exciting and it will be!).

Instructions:

1. Read the sample topic and fact below.
2. Review the various ways a speaker might incorporate that fact creatively into a speech.
3. Read over the Your Turn directions. Turn this handout over and wait for your turn to prepare and speak.

Sample

Topic: communication

Fact: 95 percent of communication is nonverbal

The speaker might employ *one* of the following strategies:

1. Translate the statistic into a literal—but unrealistic—extension.
   Sample:
   "95 percent of us could have our vocal chords donated to charity and we'd be able to communicate just as well as we do now."

2. Use a nonverbal illustration.
   Sample:
   Give the audience a thumbs-up gesture then announce that "This gesture and many others make up 95 percent of communication on the road."

3. Ask a string of rhetorical questions.
   Sample:
   "What percent of communication do you think is nonverbal? 5 percent? Wrong. 25 percent? Wrong again. 75 percent? Wrong still. 95 percent of communication is nonverbal."

4. Use an analogy—comparing the stat with something concrete.

   Sample:

   "Only 5 percent of SunnyD® is actual fruit juice. The same is true of communication: only 5 percent of it is what you thought you were getting—verbal communication. The rest is nonverbal. And, like the ingredients in SunnyD®, that 95 percent remains a mystery."

Think About It . . .

Which of the above strategies would only work in a speech and not in an essay?

Your Turn

Your goal is to impart a fact in such a way that it has impact. But you are also expected to develop the topic. To clearly organize your analysis of the topic, you may want to plug into one of the signposting strategies you previously learned.

Instructions:

1. Pull 3 topic strips from the envelope.
2. Select 1 topic strip for your speech and return all 3 strips back into the envelope.
3. Note that each topic is attached to a random fact that you are expected to include in your speech.
4. Take 2 minutes to prepare your speech—you may make notes on a 3 x 5 card.
5. Deliver an impromptu speech on the topic. (You have 5 minutes to speak.)
6. Strive to incorporate the fact into your speech in a creative, memorable way as demonstrated on the first page of this handout.

Here's what you will be assessed on:

Actual Factual Grading Criteria			
	Incomplete	Good	Exceptional!
Development of topic	–	√	+
Use of actual/factual technique for impact	–	√	+

Actual Factual Impromptu Speech Sample Topics

The following topics were gleaned from the news magazine *The Week*'s "Noted" section that gathers facts from a variety of national and international news sources.

> 🔍 *Hint:* Reusing topics should not be a problem, since students can offer a new breakdown of a previously selected topic and employ a different strategy than their predecessors. However, if you'd like to compose a list of additional topics, 2 great places to get the random facts are: Harper's Index at http://www.harpers.org/subjects/HarpersIndex and the "Noted" section of the weekly newsmagazine, *The Week*. Online you can access this portion of the magazine at http://www.theweek-daily.com/sub_section/index/cartoons_wit/noted.

Topic: salaries
Fact: The CEO of Home Depot will receive a maximum pay of $8.9 million this year.

Topic: war
Fact: 50,508 Americans have been wounded in Iraq and Afghanistan.

Topic: poverty
Fact: Children growing up in poverty will eventually cost the U.S. economy $500 billion.

Topic: death
Fact: The world's oldest person is 114.

Topic: stress
Fact: About 300.000 veterans of the Iraq and Afghanistan wars—18 percent of

those who have served—are suffering from depression or post-traumatic stress disorder.

Topic: money
Fact: 5 percent of Americans qualify as compulsive shoppers, with men and women being equally represented in their numbers.

Topic: self-defense
Fact: A $300 Taser that fires electrified darts was released this year.

Topic: accidents
Fact: Because airports are now so crowded and hectic, airplanes narrowly missed colliding on U.S. runways 15 times in the first 6 months of 2008, nearly twice the rate of the previous 6 months.

Topic: diversity
Fact: The new U.S. Congress has a record number of women, a record number of Buddhists, and a record number of Muslims.

Topic: fairness
Fact: Only 25 of the 535 members of Congress have come under fire in combat.

Topic: childhood obesity
Fact: Chinese children are on average 2.5 inches taller and 6.6 pounds heavier than they were 30 years ago.

Topic: photography
Fact: The most requested document from the National Archives is the photo of Elvis Presley shaking hands with President Nixon.

Topic: global warming

Fact: New York City had no measurable snowfall in December of 2007—the city's first snowless December since 1877.

Topic: energy conservation

Fact: Soaring gas prices seem to have caused Americans to drive 1.4 billion fewer highway miles in April 2008 than they did in April 2007.

Topic: money

Fact: Zimbabwe's currency is melting down so quickly that the government has introduced a $10 million bill.

Topic: elections

Fact: In 9 of the last 10 presidential elections, the candidate who wrapped up his party's nomination first ended up winning in November.

Actual Factual Impromptu Scoring Rubric

Name: _____

Topic: _____

Scoring Rubric	Incomplete	Good	Exceptional!
Development of topic	–	√	+
Use of actual/factual technique for impact	–	√	+

You can assign points to the criteria if you wish (e.g., + = 5, √ = 4, – = 3)

Comments:

_____

_____

Scoring Rubric	Incomplete	Good	Exceptional!
Development of topic	–	√	+
Use of actual/factual technique for impact	–	√	+

You can assign points to the criteria if you wish (e.g., + = 5, √ = 4, – = 3)

Comments:

_____

_____

Scoring Rubric			
	Incomplete	**Good**	**Exceptional!**
Development of topic	–	√	+
Use of actual/factual technique for impact	–	√	+

You can assign points to the criteria if you wish (e.g., + = 5, √ = 4, – = 3)

Comments:

_____

_____

30. Beg to Differ—or Not: Arguing in Three Sentences Without Begging the Question

As a means of encouraging students to respond to a text, I will sometimes ask them to "read with a pencil," marking lines or phrases that strike a nerve or compel them to disagree. After they've finished the article, they then select a line or phrase that really gets their dander up. I then tell them they have only 3 sentences to dismantle the author's argument. On the rare occasion that they actually agree with one of the articles I've assigned, I allow them to confirm the author's argument—but I always limit them to 3 sentences.

Why do they need to do this?

Begging the question is the most dominant fallacy in my students' writing. After 11 years in school trying to sound like they've studied for a test or that they care about a topic, they've become very adept at filling the page with words. Limiting student replies to 3 sentences encourages them to develop an argument that's long enough to be complete but short enough to be easily tested for faulty logic.

Why should they care?

In on demand writing situations, students can't afford to beg the question. They need word economy; and, most important, they need to be certain that their words are saying something! These 3-sentence replies to an author's argument assist students in assessing their own logical development and discovering for themselves that being specific with an example is probably the best protection against fallacy and the best guarantee that an argument is cogent.

How long will this take?

Total time: approx 45–50 minutes
    Time for students to read an article or essay you've selected for them
    10 minutes to read the sample 3-sentence responses on the student handout
    15 minutes to write their own 3-sentence response
    10 minutes for peer-editing and revision

What will you need?

Beg to Differ—Or Not (copy for each student)
Beg to Differ—Or Not Grading Rubric (optional)
copies of an article or essay or previously assigned reading

What's the procedure?

1. Assign an essay, chapter of a book, or even an editorial from the local newspaper on a topic relevant to your curriculum.

2. Instruct students to "read with a pencil"—marking lines that strike a nerve.

3. Tell them that you will be asking them to agree or disagree with some of the author's claims.

4. If time allows or the curriculum dictates, discuss and debrief on the content of the article.

5. Ask students to extract a single sentence or phrase from the piece of writing and to copy it verbatim at the top of a piece of binder paper.

6. Tell them you will ask them to agree or disagree with that statement in only 3 sentences and that these 3 sentences will constitute an entire argument.

7. Distribute Beg to Differ—Or Not student handout. Read aloud the sample 3-sentence responses to the claim: "One needs to be educated to succeed in today's world."

8. Before asking the students to pen their 3-sentence replies to their selected quote, determine what your grading criteria will be and ask students to check those boxes on the handout.

9. Allow 10–15 minutes for the students to write their 3-sentence replies.

10. Ask students to swap with a partner to peer-edit for the checklist of criteria that you've designated (e.g., B.O., no 2nd person "you," etc.).

11. To test for begging the question, ask the peer editors to underline all specific examples. If none can be found, then there's a greater risk that the writer has begged the question.

12. Instruct the peer editors to return the papers to the authors to have the authors make final corrections and infuse more specific detail.

13. Tell students that they now have an opportunity to rewrite their 3-sentence paragraphs on the back of their paper; reminding them that they are still limited to 3 sentences.

14. Use the Beg to Differ—Or Not Grading Rubric to assess students' paragraphs.

Lesson extensions

- This may be a good time to review methods of joining independent clauses since many students will want to make additions as they edit. A simple comma and a coordinating conjunction, a semicolon, or even the daring dash can all be used to fuse two sentences into one.

- I like to assign points to the items on the grading rubric and gradually increase the value of the points with each 3-sentence response that I assign. Eventually, one 3-sentence reply can be worth as much as an essay. This is an excellent way to encourage students to scrutinize their own logic and development and to coerce them into scouring their paper for errors. When one run-on sentence costs as much as a nightly homework assignment, the raised stakes increase the attention that students give their work.

Beg to Differ—Or Not

Instructions:

1. Read the sample 3-sentence arguments made in response to an essay that questioned whether classic literature should be taught in high schools.
2. Note the differences between the good sample and the lousy sample responses.

Sample Claim

(extracted from Joan Ryan's, "Life Lessons on the Living Room Shelf" in *The San Francisco Chronicle*, February 25, 1996)

"Only 24 percent [of high school teachers] considered classic literature essential."

Good Example of a 3-Sentence Disagreement

I want my students to laugh at the cartoons in *The New Yorker*, to snicker at the innuendo in a Shakespearean comedy, and to catch the literary allusions in the headlines of the daily newspaper. A certain amount of common cultural literacy is necessary if we are to understand one another and, most important, if we are to fully appreciate our culture—even the writers of *The Simpsons* allude to classic literature. If it's considered elitist to be educated, then I don't mind admitting that I promote the snobbish behavior of ensuring that my students know Elizabeth Barrett Browning's "How Do I Love Thee? Let Me Count the Ways" before Hallmark sells them a card mocking the poem—it makes the card twice as amusing and worth the price.

What Does This Paragraph Do Successfully?

It's chock-full of specific examples, it avoids the personal pronoun "you," and it doesn't waste a sentence by stating the obvious, "I disagree with this quote because . . .".

Lousy Example of a 3-Sentence Disagreement

I disagree with the English teachers who think that classical literature is no longer essential. It is important that all of us be forced to read certain books in high school that we wouldn't otherwise pick up and read on our own. If high schools do not make us read the classics, then who will make sure we read these important books?

What Does This Paragraph Do Wrong?

It repeats the same arguments without offering proof or a reason; this is called "begging the question." It states the obvious "I disagree." It assumes "all" students are the same; this is a "sweeping generalization" fallacy. It also wastes 1 of its 3 sentences asking a question rather than offering an example or a reason to support its argument.

Good Example of a 3-Sentence Agreement

If something is essential, one can't live life without it. Few would argue that students could survive in today's brisk-paced world without an understanding of economics, technology know-how, and crisp communication skills. Knowing the name of Romeo's cousin or being able to recite Chaucer's prologue to The Canterbury Tales might come in handy in a hot game of Trivial Pursuit, but the knowledge is not a prerequisite for life.

What Does This Paragraph Do Successfully?

It succinctly states its position, moves on to explain why other skills are more essential, and finally uses specific concrete illustrations to trivialize the original argument.

Lousy Sample of a 3-Sentence Agreement

I agree that classic literature is not essential in high school. Classic literature is not important in the real world. You will not get a better job because you've studied classic literature in high school.

What Does This Paragraph Do That's a Disaster?

It repeats the same arguments without offering proof or a reason; it "begs the question." It states the obvious "I agree." It also insults the reader with the personal pronoun "you," suggesting to the reader—who may be an English teacher who studied classic literature—that he or she will not get a good job.

Your Turn

Instructions:

1. After reading an essay or article assigned to you by your teacher, extract a claim made by the author.

2. Copy the claim on a piece of binder paper.

3. Agree or disagree with the claim by writing a 3-sentence argument of your own.

4. Strive to be specific and you will avoid begging the question and sweeping generalization fallacies!

5. Be sure to heed the grading criteria established by your teacher; he or she may ask you to select certain elements on the grading rubric depending on what you're currently studying in class.

Checkpoints for arriving at a perfect 3-sentence argument

Place a √ by all criteria that your teacher says will factor into your grade on your 3-sentence replies.

____ sniff out the B.O.

____ beware of errors in logic:

sweeping generalizations

begging the question

____ avoid the pronoun "you"

____ strive to specify

____ catch run-on sentences

____ support assertions with reasons (Why do you feel this way?)

____ other _____

Think About It . . . Why does offering specific proof for your argument help you avoid the fallacy of begging the question?

Beg to Differ—Or Not Grading Rubric

Place a point value next to the criteria that will be assessed in the students' 3-sentence responses. Remember that you can allocate points to reflect what you're currently teaching in class. It's best to allocate a lopsided amount of points to whatever skills you've been emphasizing in class.

Beg to Differ—Or Not Grading Rubric

____ sniff out the B.O.

____ beware of errors in logic:

    sweeping generalizations

    begging the question

____ avoid the pronoun "you"

____ strive to specify

____ catch run-on sentences

____ support assertions with reasons (Why do you feel this way?)

____ other _____

31. The Rhetorical Mode Scavenger Hunt: Reading Prose Like a Pro

The more students read, the more they begin to internalize techniques and style of professional prose. Handing students essays and articles you've selected from the local newspaper or current news magazines can be effective exposure to contemporary writing, but sending students out to scavenge for their own articles exposes them to many more than you could ever photocopy and allows them to select pieces that actually interest them.

Throughout the year, I strive to identify the rhetorical modes of the pieces we read in class. Even if you haven't collected and distributed detailed examples of all 14 modes listed on the student handout, odds are that you've indicated when a piece of assigned reading is satirical or when it's speculating on causes or effects. It's safe to say that even limiting the hunt to 3 or 4 different modes would be plenty to get students reading with an eye and ear to the style and structure of the argument.

I tell my students that my favorite part of the newspaper is the sports page. Yet, with the exception of a once-a-year outing to a baseball game, I am not a sports fan. I am a fan, however, of good writing. I explain that sportswriters have to be especially creative since for them only the names and the dates change; some teams win and others lose—the story stays the same. Their job as writers is to make those stories fresh and interesting every day. That's why I read the sports page. Vivid narratives, creative analogies, original organizational patterns abound. If I'm looking for a sample comparison-contrast essay to share with a class, the first place I turn is the sports page; if I'm looking for a division or classification essay, to the sports section I go.

By that same token, popular magazines and nonacademic publications are great resources to demonstrate the abundance of rhetorical modes. If I want to assign a sample process-and-analysis essay, other than the tired one in our writing text-book, I rifle through my daughter's fashion magazines, although it's unlikely that I'll ever be able to top the article extracted by one of my students for his scavenger hunt project, "How to Walk Like a Prom Queen"—taken from his sister's *Seventeen* magazine. Ironically, the student was running for prom king that year, and his paragraph of analysis provided hysterical tongue-in-cheek enthusiasm for his topic.

Why do they need to do this?

So much of what we teach about writing seems remote from the students' real world. If we can demonstrate that the strategies and techniques we're promoting occur in the sports magazine they read or the health and beauty page of their favorite fashion magazine, then they will begin to see that good writing is not a futile academic expectation. People actually get paid to write well. What's more, if you invite them to work on their paragraphs of analysis during class time, you can set the stopwatch and simulate the thrill of both on demand reading and writing.

Why should they care?

Analytical reading is demanded on most high stakes tests like the SAT and AP exams. Often students are expected to read an entire essay and offer a full-length essay of analysis in return. Coming to understand some of the different ways to organize an argument for impact is a sophisticated step in the composition process. Furthermore, exposing juniors and seniors to the various organizational patterns of the essay will prepare them for their basic college composition course.

How long will this take?

Total time: 90–100 minutes plus homework time

    Allow 45–50 minutes to introduce the project

    Allow another 45–50 minutes to work on a segment of the project in class and to conduct a peer review session

    The project itself is an ongoing homework assignment that can span 2–3 weeks

What will you need?

Day One

The Rhetorical Mode Scavenger Hunt (copy for each student)

copy of a local newspaper, news magazine, and sports or fashion magazine

assortment of old newspapers

Day Two

The Rhetorical Mode Scavenger Hunt (from Day One)

Rhetorical Modes and Their Criteria (copy for each student)

The Rhetorical Mode Scavenger Hunt Paragraph of Analysis Peer Review (copy for each student)

Cross-Curricular Writing Analysis (copy for each student) optional

editorials and essays students have clipped from magazines and newspapers

What's the procedure?

Day One

1. Announce that the class will be conducting a scavenger hunt; before they get too excited, let them know that they will be scavenging through newspapers and magazines for different rhetorical patterns. Guaranteed, the cheering will die down.

2. Begin by reviewing the various rhetorical modes you've exposed them to throughout the year.

> 🔍 *Hint:* I like to begin with a retrospective of what we've read thus far in the semester and how I would classify the rhetorical mode of each essay or article. In the process, I point out that several essays or articles we've read employ more than one organizational pattern. For instance, a cause-and-effect essay may also engage in a long narrative opening. In discussing this healthy confusion over the mixture of modes, I reassure my students about two things:
> - They've been exposed to these modes previously, many times over.
> - There is no absolute answer in determining what rhetorical mode a piece is written in—we only need to be prepared to offer proof and reasons that a piece of prose is the mode we say it is.

3. Distribute Rhetorical Mode Scavenger Hunt. Review the procedural steps for the hunt, emphasizing the importance of collecting real newspapers and magazines—no electronic sources will be accepted. This reduces the temptation to perform an Internet search for "process-analysis essay" and print a copy of an essay labeled as such for a college comp course. It also eliminates the risk of "friendly file sharing" among students.

4. Demonstrate how you could locate the 5 articles needed for a successful hunt in a matter of minutes by displaying a sample newspaper, a news magazine, and a sports or fashion magazine. Based on headlines alone, you should be able to locate 5 different modes. I sometimes like to challenge myself and use just that day's newspaper—sight unseen. I then explain that locating the different persuasive models is the easy part—writing about them in a way that makes sense will take some time.

> ○ *Hint:* This is an excellent time to steer them away from the news analysis pieces in both the newspaper and the magazines. Many will be drawn to these stories as examples of cause and effect.

> ✒ *Peter Prickly:* This front-page story about why gas prices are so high sounds like a cause-and-effect essay to me.
>
> *Mrs. Snippy:* Technically you are right—the news piece may be discussing the causes and effects of a topic, but the writer's purpose is not to persuade; it's to inform—that's an important difference.

5. Spend the end of the period with newspapers strewn about the students' desks, inviting students to find the persuasive pieces of writing. If nothing more, this assignment should teach students the difference between opinion and news. Many students have never realized that there's an editorial page or syndicated sports and business columns that appear alongside the news stories. Making them aware of this distinction is a valuable endeavor.

6. Although they will eventually be locating 5 different pieces of persuasion by the project's end, assign the students to locate just 1 persuasive article or essay for the next class. Tell them not to concern themselves with what mode the piece is written in, only that the piece of writing is opinion, not news analysis.

7. Remind the students to bring both their clipped piece of persuasion and their Scavenger Hunt handout to the next class.

> ○ *Hint:* If you fear that this homework assignment is too broad and gives the students too many overwhelming choices, you may want to focus their first hunt on just the evaluative mode by instructing them to clip a full-length movie or theater review. These are plentiful in most newspapers and magazines and are guaranteed to be both persuasive and fit the mode criteria of the evaluative essay.

Day Two

1. Distribute Rhetorical Modes and Their Criteria and explain that this is a distillation of the characteristics of each rhetorical mode that will be fair game in their hunt.

2. Explain that today's task involves them using these criteria to determine the rhetorical mode of the piece of writing they brought to class.

3. Point out that the added bonus of today's activity: by the end of the period, they

will have 1/5 of their project finished!

4. Encourage students to read their articles with a pencil and to first note the author's purpose, then determine the mode.

5. Remind them that in writing their analysis they should follow Step 4 on The Rhetorical Mode Scavenger Hunt and that they should pay special attention to linking the author's purpose to his or her mode.

6. Allow 20 minutes for students to write their hearty paragraphs of analysis.

7. Distribute copies of The Rhetorical Mode Scavenger Hunt Paragraph of Analysis Peer Review and review the criteria.

8. Ask students to swap their paragraphs of analysis with a partner and to use the peer-review sheet to assess the paragraphs.

9. If time allows, ask students who believe they've assessed perfect paragraphs to volunteer to read those paragraphs aloud for a few bonus points, enabling the rest of the class to hear some first-rate analysis.

Lesson extensions

- As the ongoing homework project proceeds, I pause, often at the end of class periods, to point out an editorial or two in the local paper that employs one of the modes. Inevitably, several students will then flock to the same article as a guaranteed bet. I don't mind if they run home and clip the articles that I've selected from the newspaper since they ultimately still must prove to me in hearty paragraphs of analysis that the article is the type of essay they claim it is.

- Students can be asked to swap scavenger hunt articles and to extract claims they can then respond to in 3 sentences as explained in the previous lesson, Beg to Differ—Or Not.

- These scavenger hunts can provide you with excellent resources for persuasive pieces for next year's class. Offer students a few extra credit points if you can keep their hunts as samples for next year's students. Having a collection of sample scavenger hunts available helps students see the variety of articles and sources available to them and provides them with the opportunity to read student analyses of varying quality.

- To make one final connection between this project and the world outside the English classroom, ask students to select a piece of writing from another class (e.g., a history essay, a lab report, etc.) and to complete an analysis of it using the Cross-Curricular Writing Analysis student handout. You can then ask students to include this piece of writing and its accompanying analysis in their writing portfolios.

The Rhetorical Mode Scavenger Hunt

Instructions: Locate 5 of the following rhetorical modes of discourse you have been exposed to this year in class. Then follow the Steps to Successful Scavenging outlined below.

Rhetorical Modes

1. Allegory
2. Analogy
3. Cause/Effect
4. Classification
5. Classical Argument
6. Comparison/Contrast
7. Definition
8. Division
9. Evaluative
10. Example/Illustration
11. Personal Narrative/ Reflective
12. Process Analysis
13. Satire

Steps to Successful Scavenging

1. Cut out articles from magazines or newspapers—no photocopies. **No electronic sources!** You must risk paper cuts and ink stains to do this assignment.
2. On each article, neatly write the title, date, and page number(s) of the source (e.g., *San Francisco Chronicle*, 3/10/08, pp. D4–7). This will help you keep track of your sources.
3. Keep a record of the source information and prepare a list of works cited for the last page of the hunt.
4. Remember http://owl.english.purdue.edu/owl/resource/557/01/offers you free help 24/7 with MLA formatting and style.
5. Respond in a hearty paragraph (about 200 words) explaining *why* this is the type of essay you say it is.

- Be sure to consult your class notes, the rhetorical mode criteria handout, and even the Internet for specific criteria.
- Be sure to use at least one quote from the article in your analysis as proof that the essay meets the criteria.
- If you're going for the A, be certain to link the author's purpose to his or her mode by answering the question: "How does the author's organizational pattern enhance his or her purpose?"

6. If you manage to locate a piece employing a combination of modes, that's fine (and typical). Just be sure you note it as such; then analyze the article's dominant mode.

7. **Be resourceful!** The library is glad to give you its leftover newspapers; your parents, grandparents, and retired neighbors will gladly cut out their favorite editorials and save them for you. I will gladly let you peruse the box of old scavenger hunts or answer if an article you've clipped is news or persuasion. I will not help you scavenge or identify modes—as long as you can prove (in writing) that an article is the mode you say it is, you are going to do fine on this project!

8. **Beware:** news stories are *not* rhetorical. The articles you clip must have a thesis (implied or stated) being asserted. Being able to distinguish fact from fiction in the media is the primary goal of this assignment!

Evaluation

Your Rhetorical Mode Scavenger Hunt will be graded using the rubric on the following page. This form *must* be attached to your project on the due date:

_____!

Name: _____

The Rhetorical Mode Scavenger Hunt Grading Rubric					
Located and accurately identified 5 modes	10	20	30	40	50
recorded source information on the article					
Analyzed articles and did the following	10	20	30	40	50
explain why the article is a particular mode					
reference to specific criteria for that rhetorical mode					
use at least 1 quote from the article as proof of its mode					
indicate the author's purpose					
establish a link between the author's purpose and the mode					
(answers: "How did this mode enhance the author's purpose?")					
Compiled a list of works cited the MLA way	8	11	14	17	20
	(120 points possible)				

Comments:

_____

THIS FORM MUST BE ATTACHED TO YOUR PROJECT ON THE DUE DATE: _____

Rhetorical Modes and Their Criteria

1. **Allegory**

   The function of allegory is to point to truths or generalizations about human nature or to prove a point indirectly.

   In an allegory, the writer . . .

   - Tells a story
   - Speaks figuratively, using fictional figures, actions, places, and situations to represent other, often larger, truths
   - Ends the story with a moral or teachable moment
   - Almost always reveals the thesis through a didactic tone

2. **Analogy**

   The function of an analogy is to convince by comparison.

   In an analogy, the writer . . .

   - Compares an abstract concept or a complicated subject with something concrete or familiar
   - Implies a thesis through the comparison
   - Conveys the implied thesis through diction and tone (taking into consideration verbs as well as nouns and adjectives)

3. **Cause/Effect**

   The function of a cause-and-effect essay may be to emphasize the speculation of causes *and/or* effects.

   In a cause-and-effect essay, the writer . . .

   - May choose to emphasize causes, attempting to explain *why*.
   - May choose to emphasize effects, attempting to explain consequences (usually future or long term).
   - May organize the argument a "causal chain" in which a cause makes an effect, which makes another effect, etc.
   - Must acknowledge other possible causes and/or effects to avoid causal fallacy or faulty logic.

4. **Classification**

The function of a classification essay is to sort items into categories—usually to point out never-before-considered similarities or differences.

In a classification essay, the writer . . .

- Sorts items into categories (e.g., my students can be classified as scholars, smooth talkers, and slackers). The categories should be:
  - consistent and mutually exclusive
  - account for all the members of your subject class
- Asserts a thesis by the conclusion of the essay (e.g., only the scholars will pass the final exam).

5. **Classical Argument**

The function of a classical argument is to promote a position with a balance of logic and emotion while acknowledging prominent opposition.

In a classical argument, the writer . . .

- Asserts a thesis, then proves it with subsequent claims and supporting detail.
- May employ emotional arguments (pathos) *and/or* logical arguments (logos).
- May establish his credibility (ethos) by citing personal experience or with research or other evidence.
- Organizes the argument using either deductive or inductive reasoning.
- Concludes by moving beyond the initial thesis.

6. **Comparison/Contrast**

The function of a comparison/contrast essay is to clarify or reach some conclusion about the subjects being compared or contrasted.

In a classical argument, the writer . . .

- Points out similarities *and/or* differences between 2 or more subjects from the same class or category (e.g., 2 ball players or 2 musicians).
- May organize the information either using the point-by-point method *or* block format:
  - In the point-by-point method, the attributes of both subjects are discussed one by one (e.g., the musicians' natural talent, their impact on their genre, and the quality of their concerts). In the point-by-point method, internal conclusions about the subjects are drawn throughout the essay.
  - In the block format, one subject is discussed first, then the second (e.g., one musician is thoroughly discussed before a small transition segues to the other musician's attributes). In the block format, the essay hinges on the impact of the concluding paragraph.

7. **Definition**

The function of a definition essay is to define or redefine a word, idea, trend, or personality.

In a definition essay, the writer . . .

- Must employ other modes within the essay (e.g., examples, description, comparison/contrast) to achieve his or her purpose.
- Usually organizes the material inductively—reasoning through specific examples then moving to a general conclusion.
- May state or imply a thesis through tone and diction.

8. **Division**

The function of a division essay is to assert a thesis about the subject under discussion by focusing on a few key subunits.

In a division essay, the writer . . .

- Breaks down a single large unit into smaller subunits (e.g., a scholar is composed of diligence, intelligence, and stress).
- Divides the subject is selectively—the writer need not acknowledge *all* of the subject's subunits (e.g., scholars may also be good looking, but this point detracts from my thesis).
- States or implies a thesis, but emphasizes it in the conclusion.

9. **Evaluative**

The function of evaluative essay is to assess the effectiveness or merit of a subject.

In an evaluative essay, the writer . . .

- Uses set criteria to assess the subject.
- Employs specific examples to support claims.
- Implies a thesis through tone—the attitude portrayed toward the subject.
- Establishes credibility as an evaluator by demonstrating knowledge of the subject.
- Dines with the opposing view point.

10. **Example/Illustration**

The function of an example essay is to enhance a generalization (e.g., students who are passive don't learn) by illustrating with specific examples (e.g., several examples of passive students who failed to learn).

In an example or illustration essay, the writer . . .

- Colors examples with rich sensory detail and vivid verbs.
- Organizes examples based on their impact, with the strongest usually saved for last.
- Reveals in the conclusion the full thesis, which moves beyond the generalization (e.g., passive students endanger their future).

11. **Personal Narrative/Reflective**

The function of a personal narrative or reflective essay is to use personal experience as a means for asserting a position on a larger issue.

In a personal narrative essay, the writer . . .

- Illustrates an autobiographical story with specific sensory detail and may include dialogue.
- Sequences events clearly with time markers such as "next" or "then."
- May provide context, describing background incidents, setting, or people.
- Establishes tone—an attitude toward the subject being described—through apt choice of words.
- Implies thesis through details and tone.
- Pauses to muse about the retrospective significance of the event(s) if it's a reflective essay.

12. **Process Analysis**

The function of a process-analysis essay may be to assert something about the nature of a process or to advocate a change in a process.

In a process-analysis essay, the writer . . .

- Emphasizes the process or the analysis of a subject depending on the author's intent.
- Sequences events clearly with time markers such as "next" or "then."
- Encourages the reader to take part in the process being described by using the informal pronoun "you."
- Implies a thesis through tone, which is conveyed through the details.

NOTE: Unless a thesis is being suggested, a process analysis is merely a recipe.

13. **Satire**

The function of a satire is to unseat traditional arguments by using shock tactics that are intended to make an audience rethink an issue.

In a satire, the writer . . .

- Establishes credibility with research or evidence.
- Employs effective exaggeration.
- Maintains control by one or more of the following means . . .
  - *Not* employing just attack and abuse
  - Preserving logic
  - Using highbrow diction and tone
- Advocates reform (e.g., "A Modest Proposal).

NOTE: An essay with a satirical tone may only mock its topic, but a true *satire* advocates change.

The Rhetorical Mode Scavenger Hunt Paragraph of Analysis Peer Review

Your Name:

Partner's Name (who wrote the paragraph of analysis):

Title of Article Being Analyzed:

Instructions: Read the article selected by your partner. Read and evaluate your partner's paragraph of analysis of the article using the following criteria:

	Not So Much	O.K.	Absolutely!
Explanation of *why* the article is a particular mode	–	√	+
References to *specific criteria* for that rhetorical mode	–	√	+
At least *one quote* from the article as proof of its mode	–	√	+
An indication of the *author's purpose*	–	√	+
A link between the author's purpose and the mode (answers: "How did this mode enhance the author's purpose?")	–	√	+
Overall rating	–	√	+

Cross-Curricular Writing Analysis Form

Instructions:

1. Secure a piece of writing from another class (e.g., a history essay, a lab report, a theater review, etc.).
2. Analyze the piece of writing by responding to the questions below.
3. Staple this form to the piece of writing and file this analysis in your writing portfolio.

Title of your piece of writing:

The class for which the piece was originally written:

The date of the original piece:

The type of writing that this piece best exemplifies:
(circle the one that *best* applies)

- Informative
- Expository
- Narrative
- Persuasive

Referring to the rhetorical modes studied in class, which mode does the organizational pattern of your writing best match?
Explain.

What was the purpose of this piece of writing?

As a piece of writing, what are this paper's strengths?

_____

_____

_____

If you were to revise this paper, what would you seek to improve about the writing?

_____

_____

_____

APPENDIXES

Appendix 1: Exercises for Expecting and Inspecting Good Listening

Many of the exercises in this book expect students to listen to one another. Letting students know that they will be held accountable for their listening is crucial. Here are some tips for tightening the reins on the listening audience while encouraging good listening skills.

REWARD GOOD LISTENING

- Demonstrate what you expect from a good listener. A good listener should be:
  - Quiet
  - Attentive (i.e., not engaged in other tasks)
  - Demonstrating encouraging body language and facial expressions (e.g., smiling and nodding not rolling the eyes or grimacing)
- Tell the members of the audience that you are prepared to reward them with a bank of points at the end of today's exercise if they have not violated any of the principles of good listening.
- Digress to tell a sad tale about a kid who thought putting his head down on the desk to take a nap was permissible or tell of the kid who munched on a package of Cheez-Its during a presentation thinking it was OK since he offered the speaker some crackers when the speech was finished. Alas, those "lousy listeners" were losers too—they lost all of their points.

Since silence does not always denote listening, the most effective means to ensure that students are actually listening and not just faking it is to ask for feedback.

BREAKING IT DOWN

- When the speaker is finished, I ask her or him to pull a number out of a basket. That number corresponds to a member of the audience in my roll book.
- The lucky number is then asked to explain how the speaker broke down the topic and tell what the most effective example was.
- Students in the audience are allowed to take notes on the speakers if they fear forgetting the main points of a speech.
- Essentially the exchange sounds like this:

Roar of applause for the speaker (let's call her Amy) who just finished.

Me: "Amy, please pick a number from the basket."

Amy: "Number 23."

Me: "Let's see, that would be Sam. Sam, break down Amy's speech."

Sam: "She talked about the pros and cons of exercise and her best example was the one about her uncle who rode his bike to work every day."

Me: "Good listening, Sam!"

- Insist that the number be returned to the basket. It's not inconceivable for a student to be called on more than once during such an exercise and for others to be missed altogether. Those that haven't been called on receive full credit (as long as they weren't munching on carrots or creating a distraction)—the assumption being that they were listening attentively since they were eagerly awaiting their number to be called!

Appendix 2: 6-Point Scoring Guide for the SAT I*

ESSAY SCORING GUIDE

The Scoring Guide addresses critical thinking, development of ideas, organization, vocabulary, sentence structure, and mechanics.

Score of 6

An essay in this category is *outstanding*, demonstrating *clear and consistent mastery*, although it may have a few minor errors. A typical essay:

- effectively and insightfully develops a point of view on the issue and demonstrates outstanding critical thinking, using clearly appropriate examples, reasons, and other evidence to support its position
- is well organized and clearly focused, demonstrating clear coherence and smooth progression of ideas
- exhibits skillful use of language, using a varied, accurate, and apt vocabulary
- demonstrates meaningful variety in sentence structure
- is free of most errors in grammar, usage, and mechanics

Score of 5

An essay in this category is *effective*, demonstrating *reasonably consistent mastery*, although it will have occasional errors or lapses in quality. A typical essay:

- effectively develops a point of view on the issue and demonstrates strong critical thinking, generally using appropriate examples, reasons, and other
- evidence to support its position
- is well organized and focused, demonstrating coherence and progression of ideas
- exhibits facility in the use of language, using appropriate vocabulary
- demonstrates variety in sentence structure
- is generally free of most errors in grammar, usage, and mechanics

*Educational Testing Service. SAT Reasoning Test. "Essay Scoring Guide" 2004. 25 July 2008. <http://www.collegeboard.com/student/testing/sat/about/sat/essay_scoring.html>.

SAT test materials selected from the SAT Reasoning Test reprinted by permission of the College Board, the copyright owner.

Permission to reprint SAT materials does not constitute review or endorsement by Educational Testing Service or the College Board of this publication as a whole or of any other questions or testing information it may contain.

Score of 4

An essay in this category is *competent*, demonstrating *adequate mastery*, although it will have lapses in quality. A typical essay:

- develops a point of view on the issue and demonstrates competent critical thinking, using adequate examples, reasons, and other evidence to support its position
- is generally organized and focused, demonstrating some coherence and progression of ideas
- exhibits adequate but inconsistent facility in the use of language, using generally appropriate vocabulary
- demonstrates some variety in sentence structure
- has some errors in grammar, usage, and mechanics

Score of 3

An essay in this category is *inadequate*, but demonstrates *developing mastery*, and is marked by ONE OR MORE of the following weaknesses:

- develops a point of view on the issue, demonstrating some critical thinking, but may do so inconsistently or use inadequate examples, reasons, or other evidence to support its position
- is limited in its organization or focus, or may demonstrate some lapses in coherence or progression of ideas
- displays developing facility in the use of language, but sometimes uses weak vocabulary or inappropriate word choice
- lacks variety or demonstrates problems in sentence structure
- contains an accumulation of errors in grammar, usage, and mechanics

Score of 2

An essay in this category is *seriously limited*, demonstrating *little mastery*, and is flawed by ONE OR MORE of the following weaknesses:

- develops a point of view on the issue that is vague or seriously limited, demonstrating weak critical thinking, providing inappropriate or insufficient examples, reasons, or other evidence to support its position
- is poorly organized and/or focused, or demonstrates serious problems with coherence or progression of ideas
- displays very little facility in the use of language, using very limited vocabulary or incorrect word choice

- demonstrates frequent problems in sentence structure
- contains errors in grammar, usage, and mechanics so serious that meaning is somewhat obscured

Score of 1

An essay in this category is *fundamentally lacking*, demonstrating *very little or no mastery*, and is severely flawed by ONE OR MORE of the following weaknesses:

- develops no viable point of view on the issue, or provides little or no evidence to support its position
- is disorganized or unfocused, resulting in a disjointed or incoherent essay
- displays fundamental errors in vocabulary
- demonstrates severe flaws in sentence structure
- contains pervasive errors in grammar, usage, or mechanics that persistently interfere with meaning

Score of 0

Students will receive a score of zero if they do not write an essay, if their essay is not written on the essay assignment, or if the essay is deemed illegible after several attempts have been made to read and score it.

Appendix 3: Scoring Guidelines for the ACT Exam*

These are the descriptions of scoring criteria that the trained readers will follow to determine the score (1–6) for your essay. Papers at each level exhibit *all* or *most* of the characteristics described at each score point.

SCORE = 6
Essays within this score range demonstrate effective skill in responding to the task.

The essay shows a clear understanding of the task. The essay takes a position on the issue and may offer a critical context for discussion. The essay addresses complexity by examining different perspectives on the issue, or by evaluating the implications and/or complications of the issue, or by fully responding to counterarguments to the writer's position. Development of ideas is ample, specific, and logical. Most ideas are fully elaborated. A clear focus on the specific issue in the prompt is maintained. The organization of the essay is clear: the organization may be somewhat predictable or it may grow from the writer's purpose. Ideas are logically sequenced. Most transitions reflect the writer's logic and are usually integrated into the essay. The introduction and conclusion are effective, clear, and well developed. The essay shows a good command of language. Sentences are varied and word choice is varied and precise. There are few, if any, errors to distract the reader.

SCORE = 5
Essays within this score range demonstrate competent skill in responding to the task.

The essay shows a clear understanding of the task. The essay takes a position on the issue and may offer a broad context for discussion. The essay shows recognition of complexity by partially evaluating the implications and/or complications of the

*"Scoring Guidelines" for the ACT Exam. 2008. <http://www.actstudent.org/writing/scores/guidelines.html> . 27 August 2008. Reproduced with permission.

issue, or by responding to counterarguments to the writer's position. Development of ideas is specific and logical. Most ideas are elaborated, with clear movement between general statements and specific reasons, examples, and details. Focus on the specific issue in the prompt is maintained. The organization of the essay is clear, although it may be predictable. Ideas are logically sequenced, although simple and obvious transitions may be used. The introduction and conclusion are clear and generally well developed. Language is competent. Sentences are somewhat varied and word choice is sometimes varied and precise. There may be a few errors, but they are rarely distracting.

SCORE = 4
Essays within this score range demonstrate adequate skill in responding to the task.

The essay shows an understanding of the task. The essay takes a position on the issue and may offer some context for discussion. The essay may show some recognition of complexity by providing some response to counterarguments to the writer's position. Development of ideas is adequate, with some movement between general statements and specific reasons, examples, and details. Focus on the specific issue in the prompt is maintained throughout most of the essay. The organization of the essay is apparent but predictable. Some evidence of logical sequencing of ideas is apparent, although most transitions are simple and obvious. The introduction and conclusion are clear and somewhat developed. Language is adequate, with some sentence variety and appropriate word choice. There may be some distracting errors, but they do not impede understanding.

SCORE = 3
Essays within this score range demonstrate some developing skill in responding to the task.

The essay shows some understanding of the task. The essay takes a position on the issue but does not offer a context for discussion. The essay may acknowledge a counterargument to the writer's position, but its development is brief or unclear. Development of ideas is limited and may be repetitious, with little, if any, movement between general statements and specific reasons, examples, and details. Focus on the general topic is maintained, but focus on the specific issue in the prompt may not be maintained. The organization of the essay is simple. Ideas are logically grouped within parts of the essay, but there is little or no evidence of logical sequencing of ideas. Transitions, if used, are simple and obvious. An introduction and conclusion are clearly discernible but underdeveloped. Language shows a basic control. Sentences show a little variety and word choice is appropriate. Errors may be distracting and may occasionally impede understanding.

SCORE = 2
Essays within this score range demonstrate inconsistent or weak skill in responding to the task.

The essay shows a weak understanding of the task. The essay may not take a position on the issue, or the essay may take a position but fail to convey reasons to support that position, or the essay may take a position but fail to maintain a stance. There is little or no recognition of a counterargument to the writer's position. The essay is thinly developed. If examples are given, they are general and may not be clearly relevant. The essay may include extensive repetition of the writer's ideas or of ideas in the prompt. Focus on the general topic is maintained, but focus on the specific issue in the prompt may not be maintained. There is some indication of an organizational structure, and some logical grouping of ideas within parts of the essay is apparent. Transitions, if used, are simple and obvious, and they may be inappropriate or misleading. An introduction and conclusion are discernible but minimal. Sentence structure and word choice are usually simple. Errors may be frequently distracting and may sometimes impede understanding.

SCORE = 1
Essays within this score range show little or no skill in responding to the task.

The essay shows little or no understanding of the task. If the essay takes a position, it fails to convey reasons to support that position. The essay is minimally developed. The essay may include excessive repetition of the writer's ideas or of ideas in the prompt. Focus on the general topic is usually maintained, but focus on the specific issue in the prompt may not be maintained. There is little or no evidence of an organizational structure or of the logical grouping of ideas. Transitions are rarely used. If present, an introduction and conclusion are minimal. Sentence structure and word choice are simple. Errors may be frequently distracting and may significantly impede understanding.

NO SCORE
Blank, Off-Topic, Illegible, Not in English, or Void.

Appendix 4: Coach As Critic: Responding Orally to a Set of Papers

For years, I struggled with how to return a set of papers: sprawl them out on the table buffet-style? Distribute them one by one, and hear the refrain "What did you get?" followed by the crumple of paper? Read a few exemplary papers aloud only to look up and see eyes rolling and attention wandering? Finally, I resorted to what I offer my debaters at the end of a round—the oral critique.

Following a round of debate, most coaches will critique the speakers on their performance based on a specific list of criteria (stock issues). An otherwise perfect speaker may have lost a round for inadequately addressing one of the stock issues. This is explained aloud in front of all the participants and observers. There is no shame, only proof of what was said and done in the round.

Timid at first, I began by critiquing my student writers' "Best of" only: "The best introductions were written by . . . "; "The best qualified thesis statement came from . . . "; and so on. Then I trod onto more instructive ground: "The world's longest run-on sentence was created by . . . , " and for a few extra-credit points the student transcribed the sentence onto the board and we corrected it. I now spend at least 30 minutes returning papers, sharing small segments from several student papers, and awarding extra credit points to the students who permit me to use their mistakes or triumphs as lessons in what to avoid or emulate in the next essay.

Of course, this requires taking notes as I read and T-score a set of student papers. My notes often look like the following:

Brilliantly qualified thesis statements:
> Julia ¶ 2, last line
> Ian ¶ 1, line 3

Most engaging introductions:
> Enrico
> Gabrielle

Vividly detailed example:
> Shoshanna, ¶ 2, lines 4–7
> Chris, ¶ 3, lines 5+

Slickest transitions:

Eva, last line ¶ 4 + first line ¶ 5

Markeisha, last line ¶ 3 + first line ¶ 4

Pronoun/antecedent confusion:

Paul, ¶ 7, lines 3–4

Shift in point of view:

Marie, ¶ 5, line 4

Alanya, ¶ 3, line 5

Before the students arrive, I fill the board with the award categories and the first names of the award winners. I categorize the papers I wish to compliment as "The Best of" and those that I wish to teach from as "Extra Credit Seekers."

If possible before class starts, I search out the 1 or 2 students in each class whose errors I'd like to broadcast. I ask their permission and let them know that the few extra points they'll receive for allowing me to share their blunders or their successes could make the difference between a "C+" and a "B–" on their essay. After kids see this as a reward rather than a punishment, they usually walk in happy to see their name on the board, regardless of the column it's under.

I'm not suggesting that seeing one's name under the "Most vivid supporting example" category on the board completely dissolves the sting of a bad grade any more than receiving a glowing ballot at the end of a lost debate round offers full compensation, but the oral critique does serve to remind students—aloud—that there is more to an essay than whether it "won" the A or not. Very often an A paper contains a flaw that others can learn from, including the A student.

> **Peter Prickly:** Hey! How come I won "best intriguing introduction" yet you gave me a C on my essay? And Fran won "the world's longest run-on sentence" and got an A? That's not fair!
>
> **Mrs. Snippy:** The essays were scored on the rubric. The "awards" acknowledge qualities not listed on the rubric—like "most likely to whine about his grade."

Appendix 5: Coach as Scorekeeper: T-Scoring a Set of Essays

Blazing through a set of essays is every English teacher's dream. But after years of being trained to target errors with a red pen, it's possible for some of us to finish reading an essay only to discover that we've written more than the student.

The beauty of on demand writing tasks is that they are intended to be read holistically. SAT I evaluators, for example, are trained by the College Board to spend as little as 30 seconds reading an essay before planting a score on it. Holistic scoring intends for the reader to move briskly through the essay, determining the essay's score based on fixed criteria. What a student writes on demand, should be read on demand.

It is counterintuitive to scrutinize a single-draft essay that was written under the gun as much as we would an essay that had been thoughtfully constructed after several drafts. Giving teachers permission to read on demand products quickly and efficiently is a must.

However, students still crave and deserve some sort of feedback for their efforts. Plopping a naked score at the top of their essays won't help them recognize why they did well or what they need to improve. That's why T-scoring, an abbreviated feedback system that adheres to the prescribed rubric, can be so effective.

A T-score is a brief evaluation of a piece of writing that includes at least one compliment and a suggestion for improvement based on the rubric being used. The suggestion should reference the item on the rubric that kept the paper from achieving the next higher notch on the rubric.

+	Score	-
compliments based on the rubric		suggestions for improvement based on the rubric

- Compliments and suggestions must borrow language from the rubric.
- The suggestions should address the concerns that kept the essay from receiving the next score on the rubric.

Sample T-Score Based on the SAT I 6-Point Rubric

+	4	-
Well organized! Good examples		Tie examples back to thesis to show progression of ideas

- If mechanics or handwriting impeded the reader's understanding of the essay, lower the score by 1 rank and note the offending error below the T-score.

Sample T-Score of a Mechanically Impaired Essay

+	̶4̶ 3	-
Clear point of view Great examples		Focus blurs in conclusion Bad spelling and random capitalization impeded reading

All holistic rubrics allow for some errors in mechanics and grammar even with the higher scores. It's when those mechanical errors impede a reader's understanding of the text, making the reader stop and start again, that the errors affect scoring.

The general rule is to reward the writers for what they did well, score the essay on the rubric, then deduct a full score if mechanics proved to be an impediment.

Appendix 6: T-Scoring Template

Author's ID # or Name

_____

Evaluator's ID # or Name

_____

Instructions:

1. Read the essay once through without pausing to mark corrections or to write comments.
2. Score the essay based on the rubric.
3. Write compliments and suggestions that borrow language from the rubric.

+	Score	-
compliments based on the rubric	suggestions for improvement based on the rubric	

Remember . . . if mechanics or handwriting impeded the your understanding of the essay, lower the score by one rank and note the offense here:

_____

_____

_____

Appendix 7: Sample Student Essays on a 25-minute SAT I Prompt

Reproduce these essays and their scores for use in your norming sessions as you prepare your students to T-score timed essays.

These essays were written in class (yes, their errors are intact) on the following 25-minute SAT I prompt:

> The Roman philosopher Seneca once said: "Failure changes us for the better." Plan and write an essay in which you agree, disagree, or qualify the above aphorism. Support your position with reasoning and examples taken from your reading, studies, experiences, or observations.

The essays were then T-scored by fellow students.

JM: SAMPLE ESSAY

IPODs Don't Fall In Toilets For No Reason

Michael Jordan once said, "My failures have taught me how to succeed." Michael Jordan is arguably the most successful basketball player ever to play the game, but he has also failed much more than the average basketball player. Although some would say that failure does not help, I disagree because failure shows an individual his or her flaws and helps that person to change their ways.

Failure creates better people because it humbles people. My friend Jerry is a great baseball player. I've played baseball with him ever since we were little. He used to be a real trash-talker, He would always tell the players on the other team how he was gonna get them out and that there was no way that they would get on base. Awhile back, in our semi-final game, we were up by one run and there was one out and it was the last inning. He was talking more than usual this game. There was a lot of pressure because the bases were loaded. There was a grounder up the right side and the second baseman got it and tossed it to Jerry at second. He grabbed it for the out at second and threw it at first to turn two, but the ball stuck in his hand for just a split second. He threw the ball in the dirt and two unearned runs ended up scoring;

when the game should have been over. We lost. From that moment on, Jerry has not talked one word of trash. He also seems to play better now as well; because he us more focused on the game and not just in getting into the other team's heads.

Failure teaches us more lessons than succeeding does. Recently, I dropped my IPOD in the toilet and it is now broken. I had it wedged in between my boxers and my stomach. Somehow it ended up getting in the air and I was frantically grasping for it with both hands. I looked like a fire juggler who started his trick and then realized that he actually couldn't handle the fire torches. Then it fell through both my hands and PLUNCK! It fell straight into the toilet. I failed to protect my IPOD. Since I have decided to not only groan and pout about the incident, I've learned something from it. Now I have the story and not only can I learn from this experience so that I never drop a valuable in the toilet, but I can tell others; to prevent them from using valuables while near the toilet.

Failure makes us better people, but success teaches us nothing. So then how is failure failing? Failure is only failing if we do not learn anything from the incident, if I didn't learn anything from dropping my IPOD into the toilet, then I would have failed. I succeeded however because I learned something from the experience. Failure teaches us great lessons and helps us to live out greater more knowledgeable lives. Failure is the reason for success, so we should all open our eyes and learn from our mistakes.

JM (HIGH SCORE)

1st reader

+	6	-
Vivid supporting examples! Strong critical thinking Well-drawn conclusion	A few slips in grammar	

2nd reader

+	6	-
Great examples!		Could use more variety
Loved the title!		in sentence structure
Focused!		

EN Sample Essay

Yay! I Failed!

It is commonly known that everyone learns from their mistakes. Although failure may sometimes seem so extreme and embarassing to actually be positive, it is nevertheless a trigger for comparison between success and failure, improvement, and therefore a means of change.

Sometimes the humiliation of failure may seem to be the focus of the situation. In terms of embarrassment, recently resigned governor of New York, Eliot Spitzer, was caught engaging with a prostitute after dutifully rallying for morality for years. Although it may seem that his life, career, and family are over, he still has some hope. He can take his failure and change.

Perfect is boring. Not being a failure once in a while causes no substance in a personality. As a child, I was often called miss perfect, and I hated it. It gave no room for me to improve. Therefore, being failing is a way to compare the good and the bad.

After comparing being a failure with success, it is easy to reflect, and change. After doing horribly on an AP exam one year, but then scoring a 5 the next year, it is easy to reflect on what was improved, and try to focus on remaining consistent in success. Failure betters the world by allowing people to change to improve.

Failure brings variety and variety is a means of comparison which leaves room for improvement. Failure is nothing to be ashamed of and should be accepted in our society as a tool for comparison, change, and improvement.

EN (MIDDLE SCORE)

1st reader

+	4	-
Clear response to the prompt	Repetitive reasons	
Adequate examples	Too many subject/verb	
Well organized	agreement errors	
Clear critical thinking		

2nd reader

+	4	-
Well-developed thesis	Several awkward sentences	
Good examples	Intro a bit confusing	

PC SAMPLE ESSAY

Bloody Knuckles

I was 13 years old, at the time in seventh grade, a period where popularity reigned supreme and the hierarchy of "cool" was the only thing on my young little mind. At my particular middle school recess time was entirely dominated by one activity if you wanted to be cool you had to get good at that game; the game of bloody knuckles. I was not a particularly physical kid, I would have preferred to play Stratego or Risk, but nonetheless I had the strong desire to be cool so on a bright sunny day when the group of cool kids asked me to join them I was very excited. Shortly after I realized that my excitement was a false hope as I was brutally maimed by the joyfull crowd of cool boys. However out of this abismol failure I took new resolve to find my own identity and pursue a better game. Although failure can lead people through hard times the lessons learned will benefit you infinitely.

Al Gore learned this lesson in the 2000 election when his victory was wretched from his hands by the electoral college system. It was this resolve that lead him to the winning of a nobel prize.

During the early 1900's America experienced a period of depression called the great depression. However out of this era came a strong leader. Franklin D. Roosevelt whose New Deal policy is a standard for the worlds industrial policy. While failure may make life a little cumbersome it is this hard work that gives us the necessary lessons to do great. We should look at failure not as an end all be all of our existence and take it rather as an opportunity to succeed.

PC (LOW SCORE)

1st reader

+	3	-
Funny!		Could be more focused
Clear thesis		Needs more examples
		Draw a conclusion

2nd reader

+	3	-
Good viewpoint		Could develop thesis more
Some examples		Provide more analysis of examples
		Points could be linked
		together more

Appendix 8: Sample Student Essays on a 45-minute Literary Prompt

Reproduce these essays and their scores for use in your norming sessions as you prepare your students to T-score timed essays.

These essays were written in class (yes, the errors are not typos) and served as both a quiz of sorts that proved to me that they read a novel and that they could write a more thoroughly developed timed essay.

My students had the choice of reading Tim O'Brien's *The Things They Carried*, Eli Weisel's *Night*, or John Hersey's *Hiroshima*. We had not discussed the novels yet, but I had told them to read with a pencil, noting examples n the text of when truth or lies came into question.

The prompt sheet is extensive and tests knowledge from previous lessons on punctuating titles, incorporating aphorisms, roadmapping, and, of course, essay writing!

The prompt sheet could be tailored to fit any novel being studied by your classes.

The essays were then T-scored by fellow students. A high-, medium-, and low-performance sample student essays addressing Tim O'Brien's *The Things They Carried* appear with their T-scores.

Name: _____

A Literary Essay on the Nonfiction Novel

What a Novel Idea!

Has the Novelty Worn Off Yet?

FIRST THINGS FIRST . . .

Title and Author of the Nonfiction novel you read:
(Yes, spelling and punctuation count.)

_____

_____

Record the 3 aphorisms from your book that you memorized:
(Yes, just in case you're wondering, this was listed on the assignment sheet as homework.)

1. _____

_____ .

2. _____

_____ .

3. _____

_____ .

PROMPT

As you've been reading your most recent novel, I've asked you to keep in mind that what you're reading is based on a true story. Tim O'Brien argues, "Often what is written about war is not what really happened but what should've happened."

Agree or disagree with O'Brien's assertion that "story truth" is a more effective vehicle for argument than "happening truth." You'll first have to acknowledge what your author's argument (or purpose) is, and then stake a claim as to whether the "storied" version of accounts helped or hindered the effectiveness of his argument.

Be sure you use plenty of concrete examples from the text—name names, refer to specific events! If the reader can't tell that you actually read the book, you're doomed!

Use the space below to write your essay.

CG Sample Essay

Fact Is Debatable

An old man sits rocking back and forth in his rocking chair. The sun cakes his skin in sweat as he moves methodically back and forth, mumbling bits and pieces of stories now and again. Then, suddenly, a noise rockets across the street like a car piston; like a gun. The man falls to the floor twitching and crying out while clinging to the leg of his chair, alone and confused. The disease is known as Post Traumatic Stress Disorder and plagues the majority of soldiers and veterans of war. Tim O'Brien, among many others, chose to write about his experiences as a way of working through his version of the disease. He argues through his novel The Things They Carried that it's better to forgo any personal observations induced by Post Traumatic Stress and fabricate with more "realistic: evidence. Although O'Brien is able to use a plethora of concrete personal examples to prove his thesis, his inclusion of the chapter "How to Tell a True War Story" hinders every example woven throughout the story. Through this chapter it can be argued that "happening truth" and "story truth" are one and the same.

Stories don't cut it, we want facts! As stated by Mr. O'Brien himself, "In many cases a true war story cannot be believed. Often the crazy stuff is true and the normal stuff isn't because the normal stuff is necessary to help you believe the truly incredible craziness." Saying this and proceeding to then tell a war story only causes the reader to question the judgment of the writer and validity of his stories. The novel is composed through a series of tales burned into his hard drive and written by his experiences in the Vietnam War. Therefore, the entire novel is essentially up for debate. One story trails the experience of one of O'Brien's friends, Mitchell Sanders. He describes a platoon of men hearing fully orchestrated symphonies and other peculiar random sounds in the middle of a deserted, silent jungle alluding to his utter insanity. There's simply no way to differentiate fact from fiction.

The post traumatic stories of veterans of war inhibit coherence of thought. Even as Tim O'Brien says that "story truth" is preferable over "happening truth," their "happening truth" is often just as much a story as the story itself. In one passage, O'Brien asserts that "In a war you lose your sense of definite, hence your sense of the truth, and therefore in a true war story, nothing is ever absolutely true." He describes a woman coming up to him after a presentation merely in the interest of commending his story and life. However, he finds the comment regarding his story offensive. Though she listened to the words floating from his lips, she didn't understand what he meant to say. Although every telling has a different detail added and subtracted, they all represent the same story. Somehow every deviation from the original is just as true as the first time it was told. If there's no single true version, there can be no fake version.

It's impossible to tell one correct version of a story. Whether induced by post traumatic stress or merely witnesses stationed at various vantage points, all internalize differently, and all remember differently. One person's tragedy is another's comedy. Therefore, the line between a true story and an elaborated story begins to fade into nothingness as hundreds of factors inhibit the recollection of any sort of truth. Therefore can one conclude that "happening" truth is story truth and both prove effective. Though one should not being the telling of a story expecting to elaborate, embellish, and/or fabricate evidence, one can hardly expect to hit every marker perceived from an event in the first telling. Our future can expect to view our history as what we've made of it and what we care to remember. The rest is up for debate.

CG (HIGH SCORE)

1st reader

+	6	-
Clear, smooth progression of ideas		Some lines seem repetitive
Great diction—vivid verbs!		
Well-drawn conclusion		

2nd reader

+	6	-
Compelling opening		Some passive voice
Great examples!		
Very well developed		

Fib It At Least A Little Bit

In "The Things They Carried," by Tim O'Brien, the author argues that the story behind what really happened in the war does not need to be fully true to get one's point across. Although using a completely accurate story about wartime can help the story's effectiveness, embellishment is not a big problem; it makes for much greater conviction and makes the story last.

"A true war story is not moral. It does not instruct . . . If a story has a moral, do not believe it." A 100%, germ-free war story really helps if you are teaching or talking about how things "went-down" in a warzone. Trust is gained between the story teller and the listener. There comes a time, however, where reciting dates and "happening truth" are not actually remembered. The reason most war stories are told is for moral; so if a "true" war story contains no moral what-so-ever, a little fiction is necessary. O'Brien talks about a time when four soldiers had a grenade thrown at them—one of the soldiers jumps on the bomb and takes the explosion to save the others. The moral is that there is a sense of brotherhood between these men, and that one gave his life to save the others. After this, O'Brien explains what actually happened. The one soldier jumped on the grenade to save his fellows, but the explosion was still big enough to kill all of them. With the real story, a sense of what the war is like is lost. This embellishment is needed. Its also needed to make a story memorable.

"This story really stuck with me. Rat Kiley would swear up and down to its truth, but in the end, that doesn't really amount to much of a warranty." It is made extremely clear here that the upcoming story is most likely not true. It also made clear, however, that is doesn't really matter, because O'Brien will never forget it. Therefore, it contains some truth. But not the usual kind of truth—it contains some truth. But not the usual kind of truth—it contains "story truth," which is a real experience that has been twisted or molded around made-up experiences. This storied truth is much more effective when trying to develop a point because it makes the listener feel as if they were there with the soldiers while it was happening.

Using storied truths dominates over using happening truth, because it gives the listener something to come away with. If someone is to tell any type of story, he/she needs to say whatever is necessary to get the point across instead of relying solely on facts.

GA (MIDDLE SCORE)

1st reader

+	4	-
Clear thesis! Good examples Well-drawn conclusion		More analysis of examples needed to develop thesis— answer "Why?" Some errors

2nd reader

+	4	-
Good thesis Good examples Great title!		Intro just restates prompt Some awkward sentences

RC Sample Essay

Storytelling has been used as a tool to look into the past since the very first formation of communication. It isn't whether or not stories obtain truth that makes them so important, but instead the impact that they have on an audience that allows them to continue being told time and time again. In Tim O'Brien's factual-based novel The Things They Carried, he establishes that proposing slightly altered facts is the most affective way to convey truth in a story. Although many may argue that true stories should not be altered if they are still to be considered authentic, but such alteration makes stories more impactful.

In one story declared to have absolute truth, O'Brien details the time when he killed a man with a grenade. There was a star shaped hole in the man's eye, his jaw was in his throat, and he suffered immense damage to his limbs, yet O'Brien was unable to incorporate any morals for his audience to draw from the story. Indeed the story was gruesome and the audience undoubtedly felt strong emotion toward the subject of death, but the story was ineffective in that little more could be absorbed from the story other than sympathy for the actual account. Had the story incorporated O'Brien's feelings toward killing a man, he would undoubtedly make a lesson out of it that perhaps others could relate to and pass on. Without morals, stories seem to confess rather than communicate.

Near the end of the book, O'Brien describes how a young girl he knew as a child died of a brain tumor, and how memories of how much he loved her when he was younger still stays with him. The young girl, whose name undoubtedly started with an "L," taught O'Brien a lot about himself, and she, as well as the message of her impact on O'Brien stays alive through stories of remembrance and appreciation.

When one looks at the impact a story has, one puts less emphasis on whether the story is true or not. Absolute truth is not needed in order to tell a good story, as good storys are ones that contain elements that may be absorbed by the audience. Whether these elements are morals, messages, or both, they make up all of the communication stories are designed to convey.

RC (LOW SCORE)

1st reader

+	3	-
Good qualified thesis! Well organized		Examples need to connect to claims for thesis development Needs to do more than summarize in conclusion

2nd reader

+	3	-
Clear viewpoint Good examples		Could develop thesis more Watch diction too. Repeats "incorporates" several times

Appendix 9: It's Time to Jam and Cram!: Preparing for an On Demand Writing Exam

A week before my students sit for their AP Language and Composition exam, I have them prepare a personalized tip sheet of reminders and strategies that they need to review before the test. I request a copy of the tip sheet as a means of holding them accountable and of inventorying what I should cover in the final review session before the exam.

Asking students to prepare a tip sheet before they sit for an important writing test designed by either you or the College Board can be a helpful tool for students and an impressive reminder of all they have learned in your class.

What follows is a sample assignment that you could alter to suit the test your students are preparing to take.

Dear student,

I am going to make you an offer you can't refuse . . . I want you to set aside some time to create a "jam and cram" sheet for the upcoming _____ exam. Begin by sorting through the handouts, miscellaneous papers, and random notes you've accumulated about on demand writing. Then create a 2-page document.

1. On the first page list, in GENERAL terms, all of the concepts that you are confident you know for the exam.

2. On the second page, list in SPECIFIC terms all of the little irritants that you need to jam and cram into your brain before the exam (e.g., signposting strategies, the definition of allegory, how to punctuate compound nouns like "control-freak teacher," etc.).

3. Handwrite the list—pencil is okay.

4. Make a photocopy.

5. Turn in the photocopy on _____ .

6. This is worth _____ pts.

Love and threats,
~Mrs. W

An Evaluative Annotated Bibliography

TO HELP STUDENTS DEVELOP ARGUMENTS

California High School Speech Association's Curriculum Committee. *Speaking Across the Curriculum.* **New York: IDEA Press, 2004.**

> Gathered from a variety of contributors, this teacher resource contains numerous exercises for practicing constructing both oral and written arguments. Featuring both individualized presentation and group discussion activities, the book also demonstrates some helpful techniques for reinforcing listening skills.

Lunsford, Andrea, et al. *Everything's an Argument.* **4th ed. New York: St. Martin's Press, 2007.**

> A treasure trove of sample arguments for analysis, this college-level textbook provides excellent chapters on logically constructing and developing arguments. This latest edition also features a substantial section on rhetorical analysis. Includes readings from the Internet that coincide with discussion questions that can serve as on demand writing prompts.

To Assist in Coaching On Demand Writing

Angelillo, Janet. *Writing to the Prompt: When Students Don't Have a Choice*. Portsmouth, N.H.: Heinemann, 2005.

> A good resource for teachers who structure their Language Arts classrooms around a writing workshop model, this teacher text offers strategies for assisting students in writing on surprise prompts. Samples of student work accompany checklists that can be used for peer-editing and evaluation.

The College Board Online. 2005. "How the Essay Will Be Scored." July 26, 2007. <http://professionals.collegeboard.com/testing/sat-reasoning/scores/essay>.

> A site that should be visited by teachers and students alike. The College Board offers its 6-point scoring rubric as well as reassurance that the intention is to "reward students for what they do well."

Gere, Anne Ruggles, et al. *Writing on Demand*. Portsmouth, N.H.: Heinemann, 2005.

> An excellent compilation of strategies for on demand writing situations. This teacher text is especially helpful in providing detailed steps and diagrams on organizing student essay-scoring sessions.

Marklein, Mary Beth. "ACT, SAT Essays Under the Red Pencil." *USA TODAY* 25 July 2008. <http://www.usatoday.com/news/education/2004-08-17-exams-feature_x.htm>.

> Openly cautioning students against plugging into the 5-paragraph essay formula, ACT essay readers confirm that even an essay with its thesis statement in the last line can qualify as having a clear position and demonstrating sophisticated facility of language.

TO HELP STUDENTS IMPROVE SYNTAX AND STYLE

Barzun, Jacques. *Simple and Direct: A Rhetoric for Writers*. 4th ed. New York: HarperCollins, 2001.

> As the title suggests, this text offers exercises and strategies for improving word economy. A perfect accompaniment to lessons in sentence modeling and "B.O.," this text features exercises inviting students to clean up the wordy syntax of sentences written by professional authors.

Williams, Joseph. *Style: Ten Lessons in Clarity and Grace*. San Francisco: Addison-Wesley, 2003.

> A college-level text that strives to make writers autonomous editors by taking them through self-diagnostic steps to isolate personal syntax problems. Some of the more complex diagnostic checklist tools can be simplified for high school students.

ACKNOWLEDGMENTS

First and foremost, my students who, over the past 24 years, have endured my creative attempts to drill them in on demand writing. I am especially grateful to Peter Prickly and all of his associates (you know who you are!) for encouraging me to rethink and retool my lessons every year.

My colleagues—both from my English Department orbit and that of my speech and debate competition world—for paying me one of the highest compliments: using my materials and handouts in their classrooms. Your continued validation of my approaches to the coaching of writing inspired me to attempt this book.

Finally, to my editor, Eleanora, who, understanding my sense of humor, helped me tone it down to make the work less brittle and more accessible, and to my publisher, Martin, who stretched deadlines—understanding that I was writing this in between coaching debate tournaments and grading term papers.